Frommer's®

P9-AZW-914

Puerto Rico
day BY day™
1st Edition

by John Marino

WILEY

Wiley Publishing, Inc.

Contents

Published by:

Wiley Publishing, Inc.

111 River St.
Hoboken, NJ 07030-5774

ISBN: 978-0-470-49761-6

Editor: Marc Nadeau
Production Editor: Jonathan Scott
Photo Editor: Richard Fox
Cartographer: Guy Ruggiero
Production by Wiley Indianapolis Composition Services

For information on our other products and services or to obtain technical support, please contact our Customer Care Department within the U.S. at 877/762-2974, outside the U.S. at 317/572-3993 or fax 317/572-4002. Wiley also publishes its books in a variety of electronic formats. Some content that appears in print may not be available in electronic formats.

Manufactured in China

5   4   3   2   1

A Note from the Editorial Director

Organizing your time. That's what this guide is all about.

Other guides give you long lists of things to see and do and then expect you to fit the pieces together. The Day by Day guides are different. These guides tell you the best of everything, and then they show you how to see it *in the smartest, most time-efficient way*. Our authors have designed detailed itineraries organized by time, neighborhood or special interest. And each tour comes with a bulleted map that takes you from stop to stop.

Hoping to learn to surf, or find yourself a deserted beach? Planning to find the most authentic island food, or take a whirlwind tour of the very best that San Juan has to offer? Whatever your interest or schedule, the Day by Days give you the smartest route to follow. Not only do we take you to the top sights and attractions, but we introduce you to those special moments that only locals know about—those "finds" that turn tourists into travelers.

The Day by Days are also your top choice if you're looking for one complete guide for all your travel needs. The best hotels and restaurants for every budget, the greatest shopping values, the wildest nightlife—it's all here.

Why should you trust our judgment? Because our authors personally visit each place they write about. They're an independent lot who say what they think and would never include places they wouldn't recommend to their best friends. They're also open to suggestions from readers. If you'd like to contact them, please send your comments our way at feedback@frommers.com, and we'll pass them on.

Enjoy your Day by Day guide—the most helpful travel companion you can buy. And have the trip of a lifetime.

Warm regards,

Kelly Regan,
Editorial Director
Frommer's Travel Guides

About the Author

John Marino lives in San Juan where he covers local and political news for the *San Juan Star* as City Editor. He has written about Puerto Rico for the *New York Times, Condé Nast Traveler,* and other publications.

An Additional Note

Please be advised that travel information is subject to change at any time—and this is especially true of prices. We therefore suggest that you write or call ahead for confirmation when making your travel plans. The authors, editors, and publisher cannot be held responsible for the experiences of readers while traveling. Your safety is important to us, however, so we encourage you to stay alert and be aware of your surroundings.

Star Ratings, Icons & Abbreviations

Every hotel, restaurant, and attraction listing in this guide has been ranked for quality, value, service, amenities, and special features using a **star-rating system.** Hotels, restaurants, attractions, shopping, and nightlife are rated on a scale of zero stars (recommended) to three stars (exceptional). In addition to the star-rating system, we also use a **kids** icon to point out the best bets for families. Within each tour, we recommend cafes, bars or restaurants where you can take a break. Each of these stops appears in a shaded box marked with a coffee cup–shaped bullet ☕.

The following **abbreviations** are used for credit cards:

AE	American Express	**DISC**	Discover	**V**	Visa
DC	Diners Club	**MC**	MasterCard		

Travel Resources at Frommers.com

Frommer's travel resources don't end with this guide. Frommer's website, **www.frommers.com,** has travel information on more than 4,000 destinations. We update features regularly, giving you access to the most current trip-planning information and the best airfare, lodging, and car-rental bargains. You can also listen to podcasts, connect with other Frommers.com members through our active-reader forums, share your travel photos, read blogs from guidebook editors and fellow travelers, and much more.

A Note on Prices

In the Take a Break and Best Bets section of this book, we have used a system of dollar signs to show a range of costs for one night in a hotel (the price of a double-occupancy room) or the cost of an entrée at a restaurant. Use the following table to decipher the dollar signs:

Cost	Hotels	Restaurants
$	under $100	under $10
$$	$100–$200	$10–$20
$$$	$200–$300	$20–$30
$$$$	$300–$400	$30–$40
$$$$$	over $400	over $40

How to Contact Us

In researching this book, we discovered many wonderful places—hotels, restaurants, shops, and more. We're sure you'll find others. Please tell us about them, so we can share the information with your fellow travelers in upcoming editions. If you were disappointed with a recommendation, we'd love to know that, too. Please write to:

Frommer's Puerto Rico Day by Day, 1st Edition
Wiley Publishing, Inc. • 111 River St. • Hoboken, NJ 07030-5774

12 Favorite
Moments

12 Favorite **Moments**

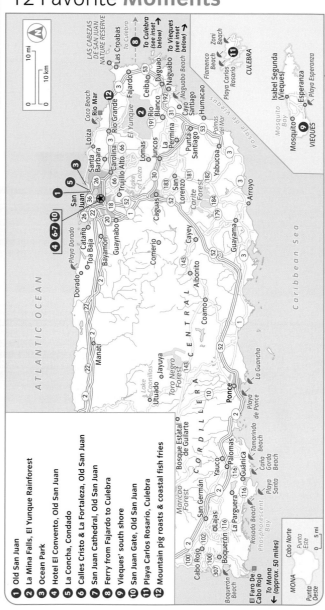

Previous page: Surfers in Rincón.

Puerto Rico is filled with opportunities for special moments, regardless of where you go looking for them, be it the cool, modern allure of San Juan nightlife; the miles of tropical coastline that ring the island; or the cool, lush forests and highlands of its interior. This book is filled with them. Here are some of the best that came to mind in recounting them all.

Swimming in La Mina Falls.

① **Watching a streetside rumba in Old San Juan** during the Fiestas de la Calle San Sebastián, when people dance, chant, bang drums, and scratch gourd shells as if they've been waiting all year to do so. See p 53.

② **Taking a dip in La Mina Falls.** The cold mountain pools just below the roaring falls are surrounded by the lush El Yunque rainforest. You won't want to go in at first because it's so cold; but once you do, you'll become instantly invigorated. See p 142.

③ **Lying on the golden beach at Calle Santa Ana,** Ocean Park, surrounded by beauty, both natural and human. See p 137.

④ **Enjoying some tapas and sangria at El Picoteo,** the tapas spot at Hotel El Convento's colonial courtyard. From there you can watch the procession of partygoers along Calle Cristo on weekend nights. See p 31.

⑤ **Saturday night at La Concha's lobby,** when you'll catch the pulse of San Juan nightlife and modern tropical style. The sleek space is a seamless stitching of the exterior and the interior, the haute and natural. With help from surrounding clubs, boutiques, restaurants, and a seaside park, the hotel is also at the center of the city's most fashionable

El Picoteo.

Detail of San Juan Cathedral's interior.

neighborhood at the heart of Condado. You'll see why at a seat at the central bar, a respite in a swirl of activity, or ensconced on the comfortable outdoor furniture, amidst the flowers and pools. See p 39.

6 **Browsing through Old San Juan's shops and galleries,** cafes and gift stores along calles Cristo and La Fortaleza. The factory outlets and unique shops make this one of the best shopping destinations in the Caribbean. See p 12.

7 **Seeking solace from the steaming afternoon inside San Juan Cathedral,** which rises skyward as if it had an affinity for the sun. The cathedral's air is deliciously cool, and the soaring space invites exploration. You'll eventually get to the beautiful frescoes and paintings, statues, and detailed facades, among other decorative flourishes. See p 129.

8 **Taking the ferry from Fajardo to Culebra on a bright, sunny morning,** with nothing but the prospect of a day on the Caribbean's most pristine beaches and a night in one of its most laid-back guesthouses. The mainland fades into the horizon as the island comes into view, and you feel distinctly remote. See p 114.

9 **Barreling down a dirt road on Vieques's south shore.** En route, you'll pass remote mangrove coastline and hidden coves fronting a delicious sea. See p 123.

10 **Walking from the rose-colored San Juan Gate on a weekend afternoon** along the bayside Paseo Princesa. The enormous entrance through the city's ancient wall was first built in 1640. The wide promenade runs along a portion of the city wall and is bordered by the bay as well. See p 13.

11 **Snorkeling among thousands of iridescent fish at Playa Carlos Rosario,** one of Culebra's most secluded beaches. See p 130.

12 **Grazing your way over the island.** From a vast array of fresh seafood on its coasts to succulent pig roasts in the mountains, Puerto Rico is a foodie's paradise—and don't get me started on the simple, yet delicious, *comida criolla* (home cooking). ●

Snorkeling on Culebra.

1 Strategies for Seeing **Puerto Rico**

Strategies for Seeing **Puerto Rico**

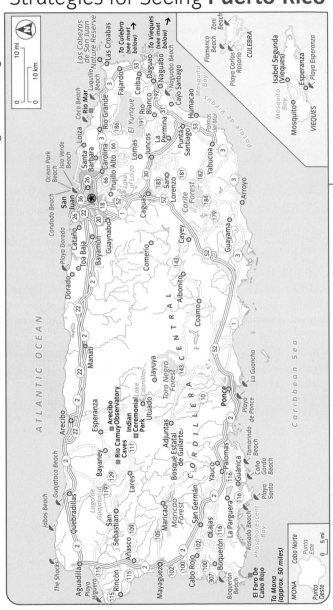

Previous page: Old San Juan.

Puerto Rico is much bigger than its 35- by 100-mile (56 by 161km) size would suggest, and it's probably impossible to see it all at a pace it deserves in less than 2 weeks. The island feels bigger because of its geographic diversity: rainforests, lush mountains, and hot coasts with glistening beaches, enchanting mangrove forests, and reef-chocked tropical ocean. San Juan in many ways feels like the capital not just of Puerto Rico, but the whole eastern Caribbean. It's a metropolitan area with nightclubs, casinos, theater, and world-class performing-arts venues, which host everything from Rolling Stones concerts and a night of opera with Placido Domingo to internationally acclaimed art exhibits. With so much to do, it's best to resist the temptation to try to do it all. Here are some tips to help you plan your trip to the *isla del encanto* and pick and choose among its many pleasures.

Rule #1: Pick your pleasures.
Don't cram your schedule, which you will be tempted to do, given Puerto Rico's many cultural treasures, entertainment options, watersports, and other activities. You're better off picking just a few of its pleasures to savor, taking your interests and the length of your trip into account. Remember, you'll want to pad your schedule with plenty of beach or pool time, so just plan to see what you have time for, and give yourself enough time to really experience a place. If you're like most visitors to the Caribbean, learning how to relax again is at the top of your agenda, so don't rush.

Rule #2: Everything takes a lot longer in Puerto Rico.
Whether you're going to the bank or driving around town, count on things taking longer than you'd generally expect. Traffic jams are legendary, customer service lines are long, and most public transportation is unreliable. Things won't seem so bad if you budget sufficient time. You shouldn't plan to do too much,

either. Island life is best enjoyed slowly.

Rule #3: Become a day-tripper.
Staying put might be your best bet unless you are in Puerto Rico for more than a week. Most spots are near enough to be visited as a day trip from San Juan, and staying in one place keeps expenses lower and is convenient. You can see all you want by staying put in San Juan, and maybe spending a weekend in Rincón out west or on the island of Vieques in the east. Other options are a night at a country inn in the mountains or a night at a guesthouse on the south shore. Basing yourself out of San Juan can also save you some money if you opt for a week-long condo or apartment rental at the beach or in Old San Juan. And many guesthouses and hotels have week-long rates that offer a savings over their basic rate.

Rule #4: Target your trips.
Don't plan on doing too much during your day trips, either. A main

The tiny coqui is considered the mascot of Puerto Rico.

Clap upon Landing

Nonstop flights to Puerto Rico are so plentiful, you should never settle for a stopover unless it's the only option. That won't be the case from major East Coast cities, which have daily nonstop service to San Juan, many with multiple daily flights. There are more limited nonstops to Aguadilla, on the island's northwest corner. You'll get a taste of island life on most flights as they are almost always filled with Puerto Ricans who have been visiting relatives stateside, or those living in the States returning home. Everybody claps upon landing, as if arriving safely were a miracle—or simply another way to embrace life in general, which is evident in almost every facet of island life.

activity and an adjacent one or two will more than do it. For example, El Yunque rainforest, a must-see for visitors, can be seen in a morning and combined with a trip to one of the fine beaches nearby and a lunch at a coastal seafood restaurant. Alternatively, you could spend the afternoon at a nearby golf course or on a chartered sail.

Rule #5: Remember you're on the isla del encanto.

Puerto Rico is its own beautiful self, from its flavors to its music, its mix of modern and historic, coast and country. You can kick it back several notches, especially outside San Juan,

El Conquistador's golf course.

from its southern coast to its northwest, and its offshore islands, the Spanish Virgin Islands, Vieques and Culebra. The pace of life, the persistent enchantment of the tropical weather, the endless opportunity of doing not much at all, is a powerful anti-stress tonic that's just the thing for many visitors. But if you want to feel connected and energized, stay in San Juan, which can feel like a fantastic tropical neighborhood of New York City, with a multitude of dining, music, entertainment, and other cultural possibilities on offer, evening after evening. Puerto Ricans everywhere on the island are amazingly welcoming. You're likely to experience this firsthand since you will meet many island residents at hotels and restaurants.

Rule #6: Do your own thing.

For every suggestion in this book, there are three good alternatives worthy of inclusion. There are no hard-and-fast rules, just recommendations.

You might want to build on some specific tours by mixing in some outings from other tours. Do whatever works. Use the book's self-guided tours and other visiting tips in creative ways to concoct your dream trip to this vibrant Caribbean island. ●

Old San Juan **in One Day**

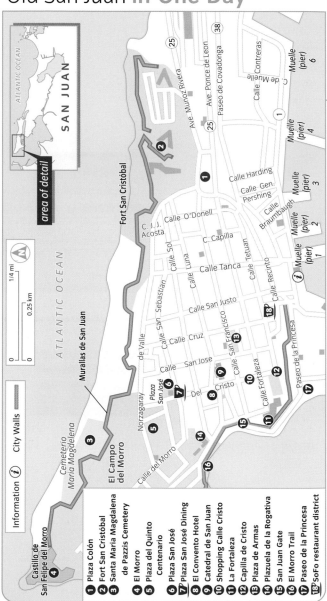

ATLANTIC OCEAN

SAN JUAN

area of detail

Information *i*
City Walls

ATLANTIC OCEAN

Castillo de
San Felipe del Morro

Cemeterio
Maria Magdalena

El Campo
del Morro

Murallas de San Juan

Fort San Cristóbal

Ave. Munoz Rivera

Ave. Ponce de Leon

Paseo de Covadonga

C. de Muelle

Calle Contreras

Muelle (pier) 6

Calle Harding

Calle Gen. Pershing

Calle Braumbaugh

Muelle (pier) 4

Muelle (pier) 3

Muelle (pier) 2

Muelle (pier) 1

i

C. J. J. Acosta

Calle O'Donell

C. Capilla

Calle Sol

Calle Luna

Calle Tanca

Calle Tetuan

Calle Recinto

Calle San Sebastián

Calle San Justo

de Valle

Calle Cruz

Plaza San José

Norzagaray

Calle San Francisco

Calle San Jose

Del Cristo

Calle Fortaleza

Paseo de la Princesa

Calle del Morro

0 1/4 mi
0 0.25 km

1 Plaza Colón
2 Fort San Cristóbal
3 Santa Maria Magdalena de Pazzis Cemetery
4 El Morro
5 Plaza del Quinto Centenario
6 Plaza San José
7 Plaza San José Dining
8 El Convento Hotel
9 Catedral de San Juan
10 Shopping Calle Cristo
11 La Fortaleza
12 Capilla de Cristo
13 Plaza de Armas
14 Plazuela de la Rogativa
15 San Juan Gate
16 El Morro Trail
17 Paseo de la Princesa
18 SoFo restaurant district

Previous page: Old San Juan Gate.

Old San Juan is home to one square mile of the Caribbean's finest Spanish colonial architecture. Fortresses, historic cathedrals, and pastel-colored residences combine with popular restaurants, bars, shops, and galleries to make this Puerto Rico's most vibrant neighborhood. After this tour, linger for a meal, some shopping, and perhaps a little dancing (see "The Best Nightlife and Performing Arts" on p. 48). START: **Plaza Colón, next to the main Covandonga Bus Station.**

Fort San Cristóbal.

❶ **Plaza Colón.** At the main entrance to the Old City, this square features a monument to Christopher Columbus and the restored 19th-century Teatro Tapía.

Walk north up the oceanside boulevard Avenida Norzagaray to:

❷ **Fort San Cristóbal.** One-half of the twin fortresses that have protected San Juan for centuries, Fort San Cristóbal is spread across a huge bluff at the entrance to the Old City. See p 19.

Continue along the boulevard running along a headland to Castillo de San Felipe del Morro (El Morro). You will pass along the Old City's northern walls, called La Muralla, designed to be impenetrable to attack. The fishing village you'll pass looks charming from above, but it's not advisable to descend as drug dealing is rampant. En route, you'll encounter:

❸ **Santa Maria Magdalena de Pazzis Cemetery.** In the shadow of El Morro, its marble headstones and mausoleums glint like diamonds in the sun and ocean spray. Some of Puerto Rico's most famous residents are buried here.

Descend from Norzagaray along the narrow street winding down to the Atlantic just before the eastern edge of El Morro's grounds. After your visit, retrace your steps and follow Norzagaray west until you reach the long path that leads to the fortress's main entrance.

❹ ★★ **El Morro.** This fortress also affords spectacular views. A park atop the walls runs along the coast, where families fly kites and lovers picnic. See p 20.

El Morro.

In front of the fortress is:

⑤ Plaza del Quinto Centenario. The plaza's huge totem commemorates the 500th anniversary of the landing of the Spanish in Puerto Rico.

⑥ Plaza San José. Dominated by a monument to Ponce de León, the plaza is surrounded by two museums and a cathedral of the same name. It's also one of the city's biggest party spots, especially on Friday nights.

Walk a short block to the southeast to reach the ancient borders of the:

⑦ Plaza San José. Several prominent bars and restaurants front the plaza, but insiders head a block down Calle Cristo for several better options. For people-watching, tapas, and a drink, there's no better place than El Convento Hotel's Picoteo (p 23).

Head to the plaza's southwestern corner and walk downhill along Calle Cristo. A block down is:

⑧ ★★ El Convento Hotel (p 38), built in the 17th century and exquisitely restored in vibrant Caribbean style.

Catedral de San Juan.

Across the street and a bit downhill is:

⑨ ★ Catedral de San Juan. This beautifully restored cathedral is almost always open until early evening, with striking artwork, sculptures, architecture, and the tomb of Puerto Rico's first governor—Juan Ponce de León.

Calle Cristo, from Calle La Fortaleza to Calle San Sebastián, is home to some of the city's best shops.

⑩ Shopping. The Old City's best shopping district runs down the street and turns the corner at La Fortaleza Street.

Turn right at La Fortaleza to get to the light, silvery blue-and-white, centuries-old residence of the Puerto Rican governor that gives the street its name.

⑪ La Fortaleza. Sitting on a bluff overlooking the bay, La Fortaleza shares its view with the adjacent convent (home of Sally Field's classic sitcom *The Flying Nun*).

Continue straight across La Fortaleza to:

⑫ Capilla de Cristo. Built to commemorate a centuries-old miracle, it is also a great lookout across the bay from the adjacent narrow plaza.

Go left at La Fortaleza to continue shopping. At Calle San José, turn left to get to:

⑬ Plaza de Armas. With a 19th-century fountain and benches, this is a good spot for a break. It's bordered by the neoclassic State Department building and San Juan's City Hall, as well as shops and restaurants. The Cuatro Estaciones Café on the plaza has great coffee and frappes.

Above the plaza, Calle San José hosts several galleries, but take

Plaza de Armas.

your first left to return to Calle Cristo. Take the narrow cobblestoned alleyway in front of El Convento to get to Plazuela de la Rogativa.

⓮ Plazuela de la Rogativa. The plaza is home to a monument of a bishop surrounded by a group of women holding candles, commemorating the 1797 night when attacking British ships mistook the procession for the arrival of Spanish reinforcements and retreated.

Walk below the plaza to the San Juan Gate, at Calle San Francisco and Recinto del Oeste.

⓯ San Juan Gate. This huge entrance was burrowed through the city wall in 1635 to serve as the main entry from the sea. Today, it's bordered by a little park and leads to a beautiful promenade along the historic city walls and the shore of the bay.

To the right is:

⓰ A rudimentary trail squeezed between El Morro fortress and the mouth of San Juan Bay.

You can go to the northernmost point where the bay meets the Atlantic, with surf crashing onto the headland.

To the left is:

⓱ Paseo de la Princesa. This promenade winds around the bay. You'll pass a shady park with stylish benches and a sculpture garden before coming to the fountain with bronze statues symbolizing Puerto Rico's multicultural roots. The promenade is home to La Princesa, a historic building that hosts a museum and Puerto Rico Tourism Company offices. Artists sell their wares along the way.

The promenade ends at a small park. Banco Popular's Art Deco headquarters towers from the northern side of the intersection. The cruise-ship and ferry docks are to the right.

You can catch the ferry here to the Bacardi distillery across the bay in Cataño. Bear to the left and walk down Recinto Sur to return to Plaza Colón, catch a taxi, or catch a bus.

⓲ West of Plaza Colón is restaurant row, which curves around Calle La Fortaleza to Recinto Sur. ★ **The Parrot Club** (p 32) serves fun and flavorful Nuevo Latino cuisine that kicked off the revival in this area. *For more on dining, see p 26.*

Waves crashing at Devil's Sentry.

San Juan **in Two Days**

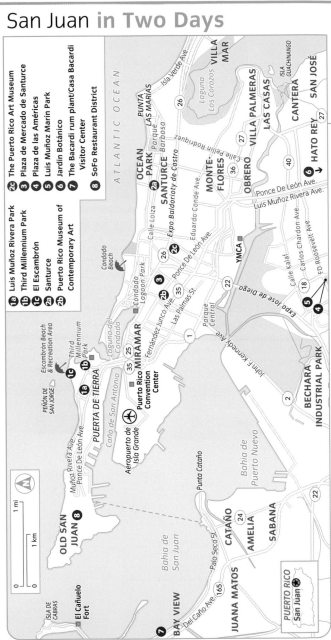

On your second day in San Juan, explore how the city continues to mature, extending its attractions far beyond its historic core. There are artistic and cultural treasures on its street and in its galleries and museums, plus parks, malls, arts venues and, of course, some of the region's best beaches. Attractions outside of Old San Juan are spread out, so you'll need a car for this itinerary.
START: **Luis Muñoz Rivera Park, between Av. Muñoz Rivera and Av. Ponce de León. Bus: A5.**

1 Right outside Old San Juan is **Luis Muñoz Rivera Park,** a 27-acre (10.8 hectare) rectangle running in the middle of Puerta de Tierra. It's now connected to the oceanfront **Third Millennium Park** and **El Escambrón public beach** by a pedestrian bridge. The park is filled with picnic areas, wide walks, shady trees, and wild tropical gardens. It also has a children's playground and special events are held frequently at El Pabellon de la Paz, the Peace Pavilion. The Commonwealth Supreme Court is located at the eastern side of the park. *Btw. Av. Muñoz Rivera & Av. Ponce de León.* ☎ *787/721-6133. Free admission. Daily 24 hrs. Bus: A5.*

Leave Old San Juan via Calle Fortaleza, which segues into Avenida de la Constitución and then Avenida Ponce de León. After passing the park and the Constitution Bridge outside of Condado, follow signs for Avenida Fernández Juncos, which cuts through Santurce, San Juan's historic downtown area. At the intersection with Calle Labra, turn left.

2 **Santurce** has two fine art museums, and one is on your right, the **Puerto Rico Museum of Contemporary Art** (p 25). Farther down Fernández Juncos, you'll go left at Avenida de Diego to get to the other, ★ **The Puerto Rico Art Museum** (p 25), both well worth a look.

Puerto Rico Museum of Contemporary Art.

Plaza de Mercado de Santurce.

Backtrack along Avenida Ponce de León until you come to Calle Canals. Turn right and go down to Calle Orbeta, where you will take a left to get to:

③ Plaza de Mercado de Santurce, a traditional Latin American marketplace with tropical fruits and vegetables, old Puerto Rican music recordings, herbs, and religious artifacts. It is surrounded by modest restaurants serving up tasty local fare at astoundingly low prices. On Thursday and Friday nights, large crowds gather as the streets are blocked off from traffic and music is performed.

Head south along Calle Canals and turn right at Calle Iturriaga. A quick left at Calle Latimer followed by an immediate right takes you to Expressway 22. Bear left outside the tunnel to stay on Las Américas Expressway. Bear left outside the tunnel to stay on Las Américas Expressway and exit at your first right for:

④ ★ Plaza de las Américas. The Caribbean's largest mall is really a self-contained city. Besides shops, it has restaurants, movie theaters, a post office, banks, and offices. There is always something going on—a great spot for a rainy day. *Las Américas Expwy. at Av. Roosevelt, Hato Rey.* ☎ *787/753-0606.*

Go farther along the expressway, taking the Avenida Piñero exit in the direction of Puerto Nuevo. Immediately to the right off the exit is the main entrance to:

⑤ Luis Muñoz Marín Park. This 140-acre (56-hectare) park is a verdant oasis of small lakes and rolling fields, with bicycle paths, picnic gazebos, playgrounds, and even a cable car that carries passengers aloft at 10-minute intervals for panoramic views of the surrounding landscape ($2 per person). Within the park, Punto Verde, a children's activity center, just opened. *Av. Piñero at Hato Rey.* ☎ *787/763-0787. Free admission for pedestrians; parking $2 or $3. Wed–Sun 8am–6pm.*

Go left outside the park's entrance to get back on the Las Américas Expressway south. Take the exit for Rte. 21, which you will take until the intersection with Hwy. 1, where you will turn left. Go left on Calle Juan Ponce de León and you will get to:

⑥ Jardín Botánico. This lush tropical garden, run by the adjacent University of Puerto Rico, has over 200 plant species, with exceptional palm and orchid areas—a perfect spot for a picnic lunch. *Barrio Venezuela (at the intersection of rtes. 1 & 847), Río Piedras.* ☎ *787/765-1845. Free admission. Daily 6am–6pm.*

If you didn't get a chance to visit the Bacardi distillery yesterday, today is your chance. Make your way back to Old San Juan until you reach the bayside Plaza Darsenas. The ferry terminal is 2 blocks to the left. The ferry to

Cataño costs 75¢ and is a pleasant 15-minute ride, affording wonderful views of San Juan. Once you arrive, take a taxi or *público* ride to the Bacardi rum plant nearby.

7 The Bacardi plant is the largest rum distillery in the world, producing 100,000 gallons of rum daily. At the site, you can go to the **Casa Bacardi Visitor Center** (Carretera 165, Cataño; ☎ **787/788-8400**) for free 90-minute tours Monday to Saturday from 9am to 4:30pm, and Sunday 10am to 3:30pm. Visitors see seven historical displays, including the Bat Theatre and the Golden Age of the Cocktail Art Deco bar, as well as how rum was made a century ago, a collection of beverages made by the firm over the years, and eventually witnessing the "birth of rum" process. At the end of the tour, visitors receive drinks at the Hospitality Pavilion.

After the tour, retrace your steps back to Old San Juan.

Jardín Botánico.

8 West of Plaza Colón is restaurant row, which curves around Calle La Fortaleza to Recinto Sur. ★ **The Parrot Club** (p 32) serves fun and flavorful Nuevo Latino cuisine that kicked off the revival in this area. For more fantastic dining options in the area, see p 26.

Casa Bacardi.

San Juan for **History & Culture Lovers**

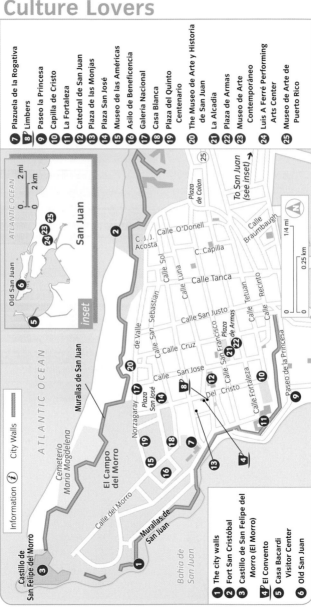

1 The city walls
2 Fort San Cristóbal
3 Castillo de San Felipe del Morro (El Morro)
4 El Convento
5 Casa Bacardi Visitor Center
6 Old San Juan
7 Plazuela de la Rogativa
8 Limbers
9 Paseo la Princesa
10 Capilla de Cristo
11 La Fortaleza
12 Catedral de San Juan
13 Plaza de las Monjas
14 Plaza San José
15 Museo de las Américas
16 Asilo de Beneficencia
17 Galería Nacional
18 Casa Blanca
19 Plaza del Quinto Centenario
20 The Museo de Arte y Historia de San Juan
21 La Alcadia
22 Plaza de Armas
23 Museo de Arte Contemporáneo
24 Luis A Ferré Performing Arts Center
25 Museo de Arte de Puerto Rico

Information (i)   City Walls

Castillo de San Felipe del Morro

Murallas de San Juan

Old San Juan

San Juan

inset

ATLANTIC OCEAN

0   2 mi
0   2 km

Cementerio María Magdalena

El Campo del Morro

Calle del Morro

Murallas de San Juan

Bahía de San Juan

Norzagaray

Plaza San José

Calle San Sebastián

de Valle

Calle Cruz

Calle San Jose

Del Cristo

Calle Fortaleza

Paseo de la Princesa

Calle Sol

Calle Luna

Calle Tanca

Calle San Justo

Calle San Francisco

Plaza de Armas

Calle Tetuan

Calle Recinto

C. J. J. Acosta

Calle O'Donell

C. Capilla

Calle Braumbaugh

Plaza de Colon

To San Juan (see inset)

0   1/4 mi
0   0.25 km

N

Puerto Rico has some of the finest examples of restored Spanish colonial architecture in the New World, beautiful fortresses and cathedrals, and museums full of fine art. The biggest thrill for arts and culture lovers, however, may be the realization that Puerto Rico continues to be a vibrant place of artistic endeavor, with Old City galleries showcasing innovative works and its cafes and clubs hosting cutting-edge salsa and Latin jazz performances. Several performing-arts venues host world-class theatrical works, opera, and symphony orchestra performances. START: **Plaza Colón at the entrance to Old San Juan. Length: 3 days.**

On your first day, take in the biggest sites: the two fortresses and the Bacardi rum plant across the bay. Start your tour at Plaza Colón, right at the entrance to Old San Juan.

❶ The city walls surrounding San Juan, first built in 1630 for protection from invading nations and pirates, still define the city. Towering 40 feet (12m) high, the 20-foot-thick (6m) walls are as enduring as mountains. One large wall runs below Avenida Norzagaray between the San Cristóbal and El Morro fortresses; another runs along the coast of the bay, with the Paseo de la Princesa promenade hugging its base.

La Muralla.

Start your tour at Plaza Colón, right at the entrance to Old San Juan.

❷ Fort San Cristóbal is your first stop, right above Plaza Colón. The fort, along with the El Morro fortress at the other end of the oceanside drive, forms the San Juan National Historic Site. It is run by the U.S. National Park Service and is also a UNESCO World Heritage Site. Park rangers lead hour-long tours for free, although you can also visit on your own, since placards and brochures are detailed and comprehensive.

San Cristóbal was started in 1634 and reengineered in the 1770s to protect San Juan from land attack. It is one of the largest forts ever built by Spain. It complimented

the El Morro fortress, situated at the entrance of San Juan Bay to protect against attacks from the sea. San Cristóbal has a web of tunnels and moats connecting its inner fortified sanctuary with the rings of defense surrounding it. Garita del Diablo (the devil's sentry box) is a forlorn but beautiful remote watchtower worth visiting. One of the fort's real charms is the wondrous view of the Old City and coastline it affords. *Northeast corner of Old San Juan (uphill from Plaza Colón on Calle Norzagaray).* ☎ *787/729-6960. Admission $3 adults (16 & older) one fort, $5 both forts, free for those 15 & under. Daily 9am–5pm. Bus: A5, B21, or B40; then the free trolley from Covadonga station to the top of the hill.*

El Morro Pathway.

The forts are connected by tunnels, but today you can either walk or take a trolley along Avenida Norzagaray, the winding oceanside boulevard bordered by swaying palms, ancient fortress walls, and beautiful coastal views.

③ Seen from a distance, **Castillo de San Felipe del Morro (El Morro)** rises from the headland overlooking the entrance to San Juan Bay as it has since 1540, although subsequent embellishments and improvements continued until 1787. It withstood repeated attacks by the British and Dutch and is a wonderful network of fortified watchtowers, moats, dungeons, and weapons and troop sites. You'll be wowed by the views, so be prepared to want to linger. Be sure to walk out to the fort's farthest point north, a narrow wedge overlooking the waves crashing into the rocky coast. The El Morro museum combines historic photographs and artifacts with written and video presentations. A guided tour is offered hourly, but the brochures and exhibit descriptions throughout are quite informative. *At the end of*

Calle Norzagaray. ☎ *787/729-6960. Admission $3 adults (16 & older) for one fort, $5 for both; $2 for seniors; free for children 15 & under. Daily 9am–5pm. Bus: A5, B21, or B40.*

After the forts, you'll probably be hungry. Follow Calle del Morro out of the fort, which veers left to become Calle de San Sebastián. Walk 2 blocks to Calle Cristo, where you will turn right and walk to:

④ **Gran Hotel El Convento,** which dates back to 1651 as the New World's first Carmelite convent and has three restaurants. The best is Picoteo, a Spanish tapas restaurant. There's brick-oven pizza, papas bravas (spicy Spanish potatoes), garlic shrimp, stuffed peppers, and more. *El Convento Hotel, Calle Cristo 100.* ☎ *787/723-9202. Reservations recommended. Main courses $6–$17; paella $20–$35. AE, MC, V. Tues–Sun noon–midnight. Bus: Old City Trolley.*

From Hotel El Convento, walk south along Calle Cristo and turn

El Picoteo.

Old San Juan.

left at Calle Fortaleza, which you will take until Calle San Justo. Go left and continue straight down until you reach the bayside Plaza Dársenas. The ferry terminal is 2 blocks to the left. The ferry to Cataño costs 75¢ and is a nice 15-minute ride, affording wonderful views of San Juan. Once you arrive, take a taxi or *público* ride to the Bacardi rum plant nearby.

5 Tour the **Casa Bacardi Visitor Center** (p 17). After the tour, you'll probably want to spend the rest of your day shopping or lounging by the pool.

6 Today, you'll see the major cultural and historic offerings of **Old San Juan.** For history and culture buffs, there is something of interest around every corner. *See p 10.*

Stay to the right as you exit the fork and walk along a shady road closed to most traffic that passes the lush tropical gardens of Casa Blanca, Ponce de León's family home, and a bayside park. The path leads down to Caleta de las Monjas and the Plazuela de la Rogativa, a little plaza

overlooking the bay with a statue of a bishop and three women, commemorating one of Puerto Rico's most famous legends.

7 Plazuela de la Rogativa.
The plaza is home to a monument of a bishop surrounded by a group of women holding candles, commemorating the 1797 night when attacking British ships mistook the procession for the arrival of Spanish reinforcements and retreated. The statue was made by sculptor Lindsay Daen, an island resident for 40 years and an adopted son.

8 Every afternoon, a house across from the plaza sells **limbers** from an open window (just look for the sign at 9 Caleta de las Monjas, right next to La Caleta Guesthouse). The frozen tropical-fruit treat is part of the childhood memories of anyone who has grown up in the city. Be sure to try one if they're open. It's a bargain at 75¢.

Below the plaza is the San Juan Gate, a rustic, rose-colored passage through the ancient city

Enjoying limbers.

La Fortaleza.

wall. Take the promenade through it and all the way around the bay to the ferry terminal.

⑨ Paseo la Princesa runs along the base of the ancient city walls on the bay's edge and offers outstanding views. Here you'll find La Princesa, formerly a prison in the 1800s that today houses the **Puerto Rico Tourism Company.** The sexy fountain at the promenade's center, "Raíces," or "Races," has bronze gods and goddesses frolicking with

Tomb of Ponce de Leon.

huge horses and fish. Spanish artist Luis Sanguino undertook the work as part of the 500th anniversary of San Juan's founding in celebration of Puerto Rico's Taíno, African, and Spanish roots.

Climb back up the hill near the Banco Popular headquarters (a beautiful Art Deco gem) and take Calle Tanca back toward Cristo Street, where it ends at:

⑩ Capilla de Cristo (Cristo Chapel). It was built to commemorate a 1753 miracle when a horse rider was brought back to life after plunging off a nearby cliff during a St. John's fiesta race down the street. The chapel's gold and silver altar can be seen through its glass doors, which is good because its doors open only on Tuesday from 8am to 5pm. *Calle Cristo (directly west of Paseo de la Princesa).* ☎ 787/722-0861. *Free admission. Tues 8am–5pm.*

Around the block is:

⑪ La Fortaleza, the oldest executive mansion in continuous use in the Western Hemisphere and the seat of Puerto Rico's government for more than 300 years. Begun in 1533, it has been rebuilt and reimagined over the centuries and today incorporates baroque, Gothic, neoclassical, and Arabian influences. *Calle Fortaleza Final. 787/721-7000, ext. 2211. Free admission. 30-min. tours of the gardens & building (conducted in English & Spanish) Mon–Fri, every half-hour 9am–3:30pm. Bus: Old City Trolley.*

Head back along Fortaleza Street and then back up Calle Cristo 1 block to:

⓬ Catedral de San Juan, the spiritual and architectural centerpiece of Old San Juan, begun in 1540 but damaged and rebuilt over the years. The domed church has beautiful stained-glass windows and holds the body of Juan Ponce de León, Puerto Rico's first governor, as well as the wax-covered mummy of St. Pio, a Christian martyr killed by the Romans. There are also many noteworthy statues, including a wooden carving of Mary with four swords piercing her bosom. *Calle Cristo 153 at Caleta San Juan. ☎ 787/722-0861. Free admission. Mon–Sat 8am–4pm; Sun 8am–2pm. Bus: Old City Trolley.*

⓭ The cathedral faces **Plaza de las Monjas (the Nuns' Square),** a shady spot with benches and statues, including a whimsical piece by local contemporary artist Jorge Zeno, in front of El Convento Hotel.

Continue up Calle Cristo and at the intersection of Calle San Sebastián you will find:

The totem in Plaza del Quinto Centenario.

Casa Blanca.

⓮ Plaza San José, which has a **statue of Juan Ponce de León** and is surrounded by the **Museo de Pablo Casals,** the **Casa de los Contrafuertes** (home of the Museo Nuestras Raices Africanas), and **Iglesia de San José,** one of the oldest houses of Christian worship in the hemisphere, which is currently undergoing an extensive renovation.

Across the way:

⓯ Museo de las Américas has everything from Carib Indian canoes to ancient Taíno talismans to island wood carvings of the saints. The museum is housed in the 19th-century Cuartel de Ballajá military barracks, the largest building in the Americas constructed by the Spanish. *Cuartel de Ballajá. ☎ 787/724-5052. Free admission, except the Indigenous Peoples of the Americas exhibition is $2, which is a must. Tues–Sun 10am–4pm. Bus: Old City Trolley.*

Plaza de Armas.

Next door is the:

16 Asilo de Beneficencia (Home for the Poor), which

dates from the 1840s and has two attractive interior patios. It's now home to the administrative offices of the Institute of Puerto Rican Culture (☎ 787/724-0700). *Fronting Cuartel de Ballajá. Mon–Fri 8am–noon & 1–4:30pm.*

17 Right behind Plaza San José, on

the corner of the oceanside Calle Norzagaray, is the **Galería Nacional (National Gallery),** located inside the Antiguo Convento de los Dominicos. It houses exhibits from the Institute of Puerto Rican Culture's vast holdings, including many of the most important works by Puerto Rican painters, from José Campeche and Francisco Oller to Rafael Tufiño and the generation of painters from the 1950s. *Plaza San José.* ☎ *787/977-2700. Adults $3, children $2. Tues–Sat 9:30am–4:30pm.*

In front of Plaza San José, take Calle San Sebastián to the west until it ends. Here you will find:

18 Casa Blanca was built by the

son-in-law of Juan Ponce de León for the great conquistador's island home in 1521. His descendants lived

in the house for about 250 years. Today, the first floor hosts the Juan Ponce de León Museum with antiques, paintings, and artifacts from the 16th through the 18th centuries. The garden is full of spraying fountains and tropical birds. *Calle San Sebastián 1.* ☎ *787/725-1454. Admission $3. Tues–Sat 9am–noon & 1–4:30pm. Bus: Old City Trolley.*

Head back to Plaza San José but turn left to get to the oceanfront:

19 Plaza del Quinto Centenario (Quincentennial Plaza)

overlooks the Atlantic from atop the highest point in the city. A 40-foot-high (12m) totem built to commemorate the 500th anniversary of the discovery of the New World stands at the center of the plaza.

Head east along the oceanside boulevard fronting the plaza, Calle Norzagaray, walking about a quarter-mile (.4km) to get to:

20 The Museo de Arte y Historia de San Juan (San Juan Museum of Art & History) is

housed in a former 19th-century marketplace. Changing exhibits by some of the city's finest artists are displayed and an audiovisual exhibit on San Juan's history is part of the permanent collection. Major cultural events are sometimes staged in the museum's large courtyard. *Calle Norzagaray 150.* ☎ *787/724-1875. Free admission, but donations accepted. Tues–Fri 9am–4pm; Sat–Sun 10am–4pm. Bus: To Old San Juan terminal; then the Old City Trolley.*

At the center of the city is Plaza de Armas. To get there from the Museo de Arte y Historia de San Juan, continue east on Norzagaray and go right on Calle de la Cruz, which you will take down the hill until it leads to the central plaza. It's home to:

㉑ La Alcadia (City Hall). Modeled on the seat of Madrid's government and completed in 1789, it now hosts a tourist information center and an art gallery on the first floor. *Calle Sun Francisco.* ☎ *787/724-7171. Free admission. Mon–Fri 8am–5pm. Closed holidays. Bus: Old City Trolley.*

In front of La Alcadia lies:

㉒ Plaza de Armas, which is also home to the **State Department,** a beautiful 18th-century building, and several great shops, cafes, and restaurants. **Café Cuatro Estaciones** (Four Seasons Cafe), adjacent to a fountain of the same name, has the best café con leche in town.

Luis A. Ferré Performing Arts Center.

㉓ The rest of San Juan also has its share of treasures for the history or culture aficionado. The first stop is the **Museo de Arte Contemporáneo** (Museum of Contemporary Art), a vibrant museum that shows exciting contemporary art from Puerto Rico and throughout the Caribbean and Latin America. *Av. Ponce de León & Av. Robert H. Todd.* ☎ *787/977-4030. Free admission. Tues–Sat 10am–4pm, Sun noon–4pm. Bus: A5, B21.*

About a mile (.3km) east along Ponce de León is the:

㉔ Luis A. Ferré Performing Arts Center. Also along Ponce de León are a handful of renovated historic theaters and a new music conservatory, which is making the downtown Santurce area a cultural hub.

The next block to the east is Av. José de Diego, where you will take a left and walk 2 blocks to get to:

㉕ Museo de Arte de Puerto Rico. This beautiful spot opened in 2000 with a permanent collection of island art that is growing worthy of its setting, a beautifully restored neoclassic structure with a botanical and sculpture garden and modern additions. Prominent local artists shine in the permanent collection, but traveling shows have featured Kandinsky, Basquiat, Clemente, and Warhol, among others. *Av. José de Diego 299, Santurce.* ☎ *787/977-6277. www.mapr.org. Admission $6 adults, $3 students, seniors & children; free children under 5 & seniors over 75. Tues & Thurs–Sat 10am–5pm; Wed 10am–8pm; Sun 11am–6pm. Bus: A5 or B21.*

Dining Best Bets

Best On the Beach
★★ Pamela's $$ *Calle Santa Ana 1, Ocean Park (p 32)*

Best Breakfast
★ Repostería Kasalta $ *Calle McCleary 1966, Ocean Park (p 33)*

Best Deli
★ Pinky's $ *Calle Canals 213, Santurce (p 33)*

Best for Families
★ Raíces $$ *Calle Recinto Sur 315, Old San Juan (p 33)*

Best French
★★★ Bistro de Paris $$$$ *Av. José de Diego 310, Santurce (p 29)*

Best Seafood
★★ Aguaviva $$$$ *Calle Fortaleza 364, Old San Juan (p 29)*

Best Italian
★★ Il Perugino $$$ *Calle Cristo 105, Old San Juan (p 31)*

Best Nuevo Latino
★★ Parrot Club $$$ *Calle Fortaleza 363, Old San Juan (p 32)*

Best Pasta
★ Via Appia $$ *Av. Ashford 1350, Condado (p 28)*

Best People-Watching
★★ El Picoteo $$$ *Calle Cristo 100, Old San Juan (p 31)*

Best Pizza
★ Mike & Charlie's $$ *Av. Ashford 1024, Condado (p 31)*

Most Romantic
★★★ Pikayo $$$$, *Av. De Diego 299, Santurce (p 32)*

Best Puerto Rican
★ El Jíbarito $$ *Calle Sol 280, Old San Juan (p 31)*

Best Late-Night Dining
★★ Tantra $$$ *Calle Fortaleza 356, Old San Juan (p 33)*

Most Trendy
★★★ Budatai $$$$ *Av. Ashford 1056, Condado (p 30)*

Best Budget
Bebo's Café $ *Calle Loiza 1600, Santurce (p 29)*

Red snapper.

Old San Juan Dining

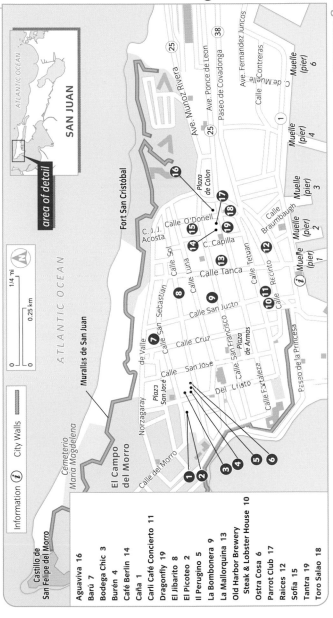

ATLANTIC OCEAN

SAN JUAN

area of detail

Information (i)   City Walls

Castillo de
San Felipe del Morro

Muralles de San Juan

Fort San Cristóbal

El Campo
del Morro

Cemeterio
Maria Magdalena

ATLANTIC OCEAN

Plaza
de Colon

Ave. Muñoz Rivera

Ave. Ponce de Leon

Paseo de Covadonga

Ave. Fernandez Juncos

Muelle (pier) 6

Muelle (pier) 4

Muelle (pier) 3

Muelle (pier) 2

Muelle (pier) 1

Calle Braumbaugh

Calle Tetuan

Calle Recinto

Calle Tanca

Calle San Justo

Calle San Francisco

Plaza
de Armos

Calle Fortaleza

Paseo de la Princesa

Calle Cristo

Calle San Jose

Calle Cruz

Calle San Sebastian

Calle Luna

Calle Sol

Calle O'Donell

C. J. J. Acosta

C. Capilla

Plaza
San José

Calle San José

Norzagaray

Calle del Morro

Aguaviva **16**
Barú **7**
Bodega Chic **3**
Burén **4**
Café Berlin **14**
Caña **1**
Carli Café Concierto **11**
Dragonfly **19**
El Jibarito **8**
El Picoteo **2**
Il Perugino **5**
La Bombonera **9**
La Mallorquina **13**
Old Harbor Brewery
Steak & Lobster House **10**
Ostra Cosa **6**
Parrot Club **17**
Raíces **12**
Sofía **15**
Tantra **19**
Toro Salao **18**

Isla Verde & Condado Dining

Ajili Mójili 2
Bebo's Café 9
Bistro de Paris 7
BLT Steak 15
Bodega Compostela 5

Budatai 3
Don Tello 1
Great Taste 2
La Casita Blanca 14
Mike & Charlie's 2

Niché 11
Pamela's 12
Perla 6
Pikayo 8
Pinky's 4
Repostería Kasalta 13
Via Appia 10

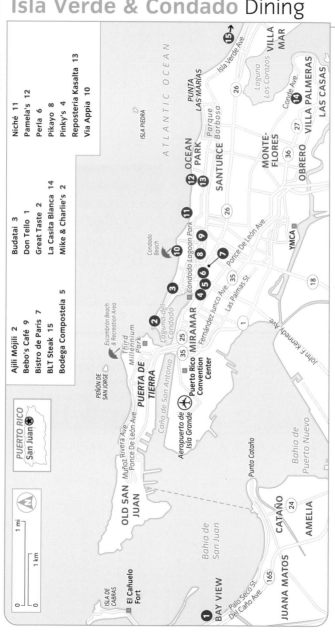

San Juan Restaurants A to Z

★★ **Aguaviva** OLD SAN JUAN *LATINO/SEAFOOD* Dive right into this chic spot that undulates with sea colors and shapes, and take a bite from its signature sushi-ceviche raw bar or its hot and cold appetizer towers. The place to splurge for seafood lovers. *Calle Fortaleza 364.* ☎ *787/722-0665. Entrees $16–$45. MC, V. Lunch & dinner daily. Bus: Old City Trolley. Map p 27.*

★★ **Ajili Mójili** CONDADO *PUERTO RICAN* Down-home Puerto Rican food done right. The restaurant also has an elegant dining room with a great view over the lagoon. *Av. Ashford 1006.* ☎ *787/725-9195. Entrees $13–$26. AE, DISC, MC, V. Lunch & dinner daily. Bus: B21. Map p 28.*

★★ **Barú** OLD SAN JUAN *CARIBBEAN/MEDITERRANEAN* The inventive fusion cuisine and the beautifully restored bar-restaurant draw a fashionable crowd all the time at this fixture on the Old City's most lively block. Dishes, sized between entree and appetizer portions, are perfect for sharing over drinks. *Calle San Sebastián 150.* ☎ *787/977-7107. Entrees $15–$28. MC, V. Lunch & dinner daily. Bus: Old City Trolley. Map p 27.*

Bebo's Café SANTURCE *PUERTO RICAN* Large portions of tasty local favorites at great prices keep this place packed from dawn to after midnight. *Calle Loiza 1600.* ☎ *787/726-1008. Entrees $6–$22. AE, MC, V. Breakfast, lunch & dinner daily. Bus: A5. Map p 28.*

★★★ **Bistro de Paris** SANTURCE *FRENCH* A classic French bistro in one of downtown San Juan's trendiest neighborhoods, it delivers some of the tastiest dishes I've ever tried. Pricey but worth it. *Plaza Diego, Av.*

Comida Criolla.

José de Diego 310. ☎ *787/998-8929. Entrees $25–$37. AE, MC, V. Lunch & dinner Mon–Sat, brunch Sun. Bus: A5. Map p 28.*

★★★ **BLT Steak** ISLA VERDE *STEAKHOUSE* The American steakhouse brought to towering heights by French chef Laurent Tourondel, who overdoes everything to great effect, including the sides. *At the Ritz-Carlton San Juan, Av. de los Gobernadores 6961.* ☎ *787/253-1700. Entrees $22–$88. AE, MC, V. Dinner daily. Bus: A5. Map p 28.*

★★ **Bodega Chic** OLD SAN JUAN *FRENCH/ALGERIAN* At this comfortable little spot, chef Christophe Gourdain delivers incredibly delicious French cuisine inspired by the tropics. Prices are great for what you get. *Calle Cristo 51.* ☎ *787/722-0124. Entrees $15–$26. AE, MC, V. Dinner Tues–Sun. Closed Mon. Bus: Old City Trolley. Map p 27.*

★★ **Bodega Compostela** SAN-TURCE *TAPAS/WINE* This fixture of San Juan's dining scene reinvented itself as a chic wine and tapas bar, but it still serves among the best Spanish food in the city (where nearly all of it is good). *Av. Condado 106.* ☎ *787/724-6099. Tapas $2.95–$26. Entrees $34–$45. AE, DC, MC, V. Lunch Mon–Fri, dinner Mon–Sat. Bus: A5. Map p 28.*

★★★ **Budatai** CONDADO *LATIN/ASIAN* Home to one of the best meals you'll find on the island, the ambience at the new home of "Iron Chef" Roberto Trevino is just as scrumptious, from the young and beautiful clientele to the view of the oceanfront park. *Av. Ashford 1056.* ☎ *787/725-6919. Entrees $24–$35. AE, MC, V. Lunch & dinner daily. Bus: B21. Map p 28.*

★ **Burén** OLD SAN JUAN *INTERNA-TIONAL* This funky bistro serves up surprisingly inventive entrees, tasty pizza and pastas, and grilled steaks. You can eat at the brightly colored bar area, in the more colonial dining room, or in the quiet courtyard. *17 Calle Cristo 103.* ☎ *787/977-5023. Entrees $16–$26. AE, DC, DISC, MC, V. Dinner daily. Bus: Old City Trolley. Map p 27.*

★ **Café Berlin** OLD SAN JUAN *BAKERY/BISTRO* This European cafe serves delicious baked goods, brunch items, pastas, and light, healthy entrees from its tree-shaded perch on Plaza Colón. *Calle San Francisco 407, Plaza Colón.* ☎ *787/722-5205. Entrees $8–$16. AE, MC, V. Breakfast, lunch & dinner daily. Bus: A5. Map p 27.*

★ **Caña** OLD SAN JUAN *PUERTO RICAN* A rum bar and restaurant in the beautiful Hotel El Convento, it serves up light, inventive takes on traditional island cooking as well as pizzas, salads, and sandwiches. *Hotel El Convento, Calle Cristo 100.* ☎ *787/723-9200. Entrees $17–$26. AE, MC, V. Lunch & dinner daily. Bus: Old City Trolley. Map p 27.*

★ **Carli Café Concierto** OLD SAN JUAN *INTERNATIONAL* The fine food tastes even better as owner Carli Muñoz, who played keyboards with the Beach Boys, entertains with romantic standards and Latin jazz from the restaurant's grand piano. *Edificio Banco Popular, Calle Tetuán 206, off Plazoleta Rafael Carrión.* ☎ *787/725-4927. Entrees $16–$36. AE, MC, V. Lunch & dinner Mon–Sat. Bus: Old City Trolley. Map p 27.*

Interior of Budatiai.

★★ **Don Tello** SANTURCE *PUERTO RICAN* Right across the street from the Santurce Marketplace (Plaza del Mercado), this family-run restaurant serves authentic *comida criolla* using the abundance of fresh herbs and other ingredients arriving at the market daily. *Calle Dos Hermanos 180.* ☎ *787/724-5752. Entrees $6–$20. AE, MC, V. Lunch Mon–Sat, dinner Tues–Sat. Bus: A5. Map p 28.*

★★★ **Dragonfly** OLD SAN JUAN *LATIN/ASIAN FUSION* This opulent Oriental lounge, San Juan's first Latin–Asian menu and one of the best anywhere, serves oversized appetizer portions, or *platos*, whose seductive power attracts lines of waiting diners out the front door. *Calle Fortaleza 364.* ☎ *787/977-3886. Entrees $8–$30. AE, MC, V. Dinner daily. Bus: A5. Map p 27.*

★ **kids** **El Jibarito** OLD SAN JUAN *PUERTO RICAN* Classic Puerto Rican fare in a lovely but informal open cafe in a residential neighborhood of the Old City. It's where locals come when they're craving home cooking. *Calle Sol 280.* ☎ *787/725-8375. Entrees $7.95–$18. AE, DC, MC, V. Lunch & dinner daily. Bus: Old City Trolley. Map p 29.*

★★ **El Picoteo** OLD SAN JUAN *SPANISH/TAPAS* Spilling across the terrace of Old San Juan's most beautiful hotel, El Picoteo serves extraordinary tapas in a sublime ambience. *Calle Cristo 100.* ☎ *787/723-9202. Tapas $6–$17; entrees $20–$40. AE, MC, V. Lunch & dinner daily. Bus: Old City Trolley. Map p 27.*

★ **kids** **Great Taste** CONDADO *CHINESE* This is where the island's populous Chinese community comes to eat for their Sunday dim sum splurge. The quality is high and the prices are low—all this with a lagoon view. *Av. Ashford 1018.* ☎ *787/721-8111. Entrees $8–$45.*

AE, MC, V. Lunch & dinner daily. Bus: A5, B21. Map p 28.

★★ **Il Perugino** OLD SAN JUAN *ITALIAN* Classic Italian cuisine inspired by chef owner Franco Seccarelli's hometown in Umbria, with flawless, formal service in an exquisitely renovated Spanish colonial building. *Calle Cristo 105.* ☎ *787/722-5481. Entrees $29–$41. AE, DISC, MC, V. Dinner daily; lunch Tues–Sat. Bus: Old City Trolley. Map p 27.*

★ **kids** **La Bombonera** OLD SAN JUAN *CAFETERIA* Homemade pastries, sandwiches, and tasty basic *comida criolla* in a well-kept cafe/bakery dating from 1902—great for coffee or breakfast, or a fruit drink, but the food is good enough to warrant coming for a full meal. *Calle San Francisco 250.* ☎ *787/722-0658. Breakfast $4.50–$11; entrees $6–$20. AE, MC, V. Breakfast, lunch and dinner daily. Bus: Old City Trolley. Map p 27.*

★ **La Casita Blanca** SANTURCE *PUERTO RICAN* If you can't make it out to the countryside, stop by this converted family home off the touristy path that brings those island flavors to the city. *Calle Ponce de León 762.* ☎ *787/722-0444. Entrees $8–$20. AE, MC, V. Lunch & dinner Mon–Sat; Sun, brunch. Take a taxi. Map p 28.*

★ **La Mallorquina** OLD SAN JUAN *PUERTO RICAN* Founded in 1848, La Mallorquina positively oozes old-world charm and serves up exquisite renditions of Puerto Rican classics like *arroz con pollo* (chicken and rice) and seafood *asopao* (rice stew). *Calle San Justo 207.* ☎ *787/722-2383. Entrees $15–$36. AE, MC, V. Lunch & dinner Mon–Sat. Bus: Old City Trolley. Map p 27.*

★ **kids** **Mike & Charlie's** CONDADO *PIZZA* With Jersey shore–style pizza that's as much about the tomato as the cheese, this joint

Hotel Dining

San Juan is for a great city for eating out, and its hotels are a big part of the reason why. Excellent steakhouses have set up San Juan restaurants, including **The Palm** (El San Juan Hotel), **Ruth's Chris Steak House** (Inter-Continental San Juan Resort & Casino), and **Morton's of Chicago** (Caribe Hilton). Other standouts include Italian restaurants **La Piccola Fontana** (El San Juan), and **Ristorante Tuscany** (San Juan Marriott), and the outdoor cafe **Ciao Mediterranean Café** (Inter-Continental San Juan), one of the best spots in San Juan to eat on the beach.

serves the best slice in the city, plus fat subs and great salads. *Av. Ashford 1024.* 787/725-8711. *Entrees $12–$20. MC, V. Lunch & dinner daily. Map p 28.*

★★★ **Niché** CONDADO *LATIN FUSION* This spare little spot inside an attractive guesthouse by the beach delivers a big punch, awe-inspiring dishes based on local flavors, seafood, and exotic meats. *Calle Taft 8.* 787/725-0669. *Entrees $20–$40. AE, MC, V. Dinner daily. Bus: A5, B21. Map p 28.*

★ **kids Old Harbor Brewery Steak and Lobster House** OLD SAN JUAN *AMERICAN* San Juan's only microbrewery serves old-school steak and seafood in an upscale tavern setting. *Calle Tizol 202 (near Recinto Sur).* 787/721-2100. *Entrees $12–$38. AE, MC. Lunch & dinner daily. Map p 27.*

★ **Ostra Cosa** OLD SAN JUAN *ECLECTIC* The food's not bad, but the atmosphere is spectacular. Dine beneath the stars and the branches of a massive quenepe tree in the courtyard of a beautifully restored 16th-century residence. *Calle Cristo 154.* 787/722-2672. *Entrees $18–$29. AE, MC, V. Lunch & dinner daily. Bus: Old City Trolley. Map p 27.*

★★ **Pamela's** OCEAN PARK *CARIBBEAN FUSION* This inventive

menu, which pairs distinct Caribbean cuisine flavors with continental fare, lives up to the restaurant's location on San Juan's best beach. *At Número Uno Guest House, Calle Santa Ana 1.* 787/726-5010. *Entrees $15–$35. AE, MC, V. Lunch & dinner daily. Bus: A5. Map p 28.*

★★ **Parrot Club** OLD SAN JUAN *NUEVO LATINO* It's fun, colorful, and extremely friendly, but the crowds come for the Nuevo Latino cooking, among the best in the New or the Old World. The club features live salsa and Latin Jazz 2 nights a week, but fine vibes all the time. *Calle Fortaleza 363.* 787/725-7370. *AE, DISC, MC, V. Lunch & dinner daily. Bus: Old City Trolley. Map p 27.*

★★★ **Perla** CONDADO *SEAFOOD* This seashell-shaped restaurant on the beach shimmers with fluid and light, the perfect setting for Dayn Smith's "urbane" cuisine, with a menu that skitters effortlessly from Arctic char to lamb chops. *Av. Ashford 1077.* 787/721-7500, *ext. 6800. Entrees $25–$40. AE, MC, V. Dinner daily. Bus: A5. Map p 28.*

★★★ **Pikayo** SANTURCE *NUEVO CRIOLLO* Living up to its surroundings in the island's finest museum, the restaurant brings the classic Spanish, Indian, and African elements of Puerto Rican cuisine to new heights through artful reinventions. *Puerto Rico Museum of Art, Av. José de Diego 299.* ☎ *787/721-6194. Entrees $28–$40. AE, DC, MC, V. Lunch Tues–Fri; dinner Mon–Sat. Bus: A5. Map p 28.*

★ **Pinky's** SANTURCE *CAFE/DELI* With wraps, sandwiches, and frappes, the new location at Bar Rubi is right near the Plaza del Mercado. *Calle Canals 213.* ☎ *787/289-8080. Sandwiches $5.50–$15. MC, V. Lunch daily; dinner Thurs–Sat. Bus: A5. Map p 28.*

★ **Raíces** OLD SAN JUAN *PUERTO RICAN* Enjoy the rustic atmosphere and folkloric dress of the staff. The *comida criolla* here is the real deal, which is why locals, as well as tourists, come to enjoy home cooking done right. *Calle Recinto Sur 315.* ☎ *787/289-2121. Entrees $10–$27. AE, MC, V. Lunch & Dinner Mon–Sat. Bus: A5. Map p 27.*

★ **Repostería Kasalta** OCEAN PARK *SPANISH/PUERTO RICAN* Serving great breakfasts, baked goods, and sandwiches—alongside Spanish classics like *caldo gallego,* a pork-and-bean soup, and *paella Valenciano,* a mix of seafood and chicken on a bed of saffron rice. *Calle McLeary 1966.* ☎ *787/727-7340. Entrees $5–$22. AE, DC, MC, V.*

Breakfast, lunch & dinner daily. Bus: A5. Map p 28.

★★ **Sofia** OLD SAN JUAN *ITALIAN* This trattoria takes you to Rome with its courtyard, arched doorways, exposed brick, and mahogany bar. There are delicate designer pizzas, scrumptious pastas, and entrees like saltimbocca alla romana. *Calle San Francisco 355.* ☎ *787/721-0396. Entrees $20–$42; pizzas $12–$16. AE, DISC, MC, V. Lunch & dinner daily. Bus: Old City Trolley. Map p 27.*

★★ **Tantra** OLD SAN JUAN *INDIAN-LATINO* Delicious South Indian–Latino fusion food is served all night at this Hindu-inspired bar and dining room. The scene is always lively, with belly-dancing on weekend nights. *Calle Fortaleza 356.* ☎ *787/977-8141. Entrees $13–$19. AE, MC, V. Lunch Tues–Sat; dinner Mon–Sat. Bus: A5. Map p 27.*

★★ **Toro Salao** OLD SAN JUAN *SPANISH TAPAS* Toro Salao has an entire menu of sangria, fresh takes on classic Spanish tapas, and complete entrees you can enjoy in the upstairs tavern, the main dining room, or the outdoor cafe. *Calle Tetuán 367.* ☎ *787/722-3330. Entrees $22–$35; tapas $12–$25. AE, MC, V. Dinner daily. Bus: A5. Map p 27.*

Nuevo Latino appetizers at Ristorante Tuscany at the San Juan Marriott.

Lodging Best Bets

El Convento.

Best **Historic Hotel**
★★★ Gran Hotel El Convento $$$
Calle Cristo 100, Old San Juan
(p 38)

Best **Luxury Hotel**
★★★ The Ritz-Carlton $$$ *Av.*
de los Gobernadores (State Rd.)
6961, no. 187, Gran Isla Verde
(p 39)

Best **Moderate Hotel**
★★ Número Uno on the Beach $$
Calle Santa Ana 1, Ocean Park
(p 39)

Best **Budget Hotel**
El Canario Inn $ *Av. Ashford 1317,*
Condado (p 37)

Best **B&B**
★ Gallery Inn $$ *Calle Norzagaray*
204–206, Old San Juan (p 38)

Best **Service**
★ Marriott Hotel & Stellaris Casino
$$$ *Av. Ashford 1309, Condado*
(p 39)

Best **Hot Property**
★★ La Concha: A Renaissance
Resort $$$ *Av. Ashford 1077,*
Condado (p 39)

Old San Juan Lodging

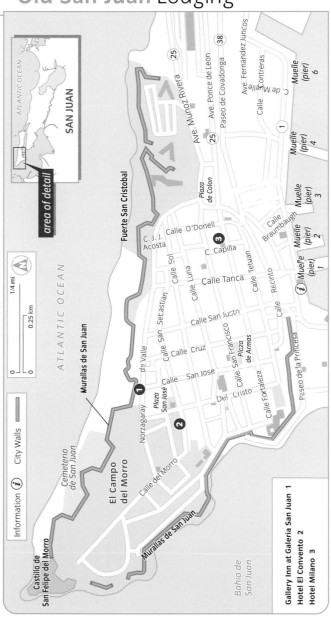

Information (i)   City Walls

ATLANTIC OCEAN

SAN JUAN

area of detail

ATLANTIC OCEAN

0   1/4 mi

0   0.25 km

Castillo de
San Felipe del Morro

Cemeterio
de San Juan

El Campo
del Morro

Murallas de San Juan

Calle del Morro

Murallas de San Juan

Bahia de
San Juan

Fuerte San Cristobal

Plaza
de Colon

C. J. J.   Calle O'Donell
Acosta

C. Capilla

Calle Sol

Calle Luna

Calle Tanca

Calle San Sebastian

Calle San Justo

Calle Cruz

Plaza
San José

Calle   San Jose

Del   Cristo

Calle Fortaleza

Paseo de la Princesa

Norzagaray

d'Valle

Plaza
de Armos

Calle San Francisco

Calle Tetuan

Calle Recinto

Calle

Calle Braumbaugh

Muelle
(pier)
1

Muelle
(pier)
2

Muelle
(pier)
3

Muelle
(pier)
4

Muelle
(pier)
6

C. de Muelle

Calle Contreras

Ave. Fernandez Juncos

Paseo de Covadonga

Ave. Ponce de Leon

Ave. Muñoz Rivera

25

25

38

1

Gallery Inn at Galeria San Juan 1
Hotel El Convento 2
Hotel Milano 3

Isla Verde & Condado Lodging

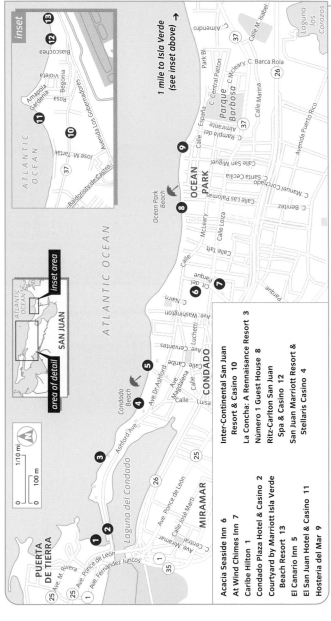

inset

1 mile to Isla Verde
(see inset above) ↑

ATLANTIC OCEAN

SAN JUAN

inset area

area of detail

CONDADO

OCEAN PARK

Ocean Park Beach

Condado Beach

Laguna del Condado

MIRAMAR

PUERTA DE TIERRA

Acacia Seaside Inn 6
At Wind Chimes Inn 7
Caribe Hilton 1
Condado Plaza Hotel & Casino 2
Courtyard by Marriott Isla Verde Beach Resort 13
El Canario Inn 5
El San Juan Hotel & Casino 11
Hosteria del Mar 9

Inter-Continental San Juan Resort & Casino 10
La Concha: A Rennaisance Resort 3
Número 1 Guest House 8
Ritz-Carlton San Juan Spa & Casino 12
San Juan Marriott Resort & Stellaris Casino 4

San Juan Lodging A to Z

★ **kids** **At Wind Chimes Inn** CONDADO This restored and renovated Spanish manor a block from Condado's best stretch of beach has an open-air patio with tables surrounded by palm trees and bougainvillea. The inn has different-sized rooms with kitchens; all are comfortable and pretty. Its sister property down the street, **Acacia Seaside Inn** (Calle Taft 8; ☎ 787/725-0668; www.acacia seasideinn.com), is also highly recommended. *Av. McLeary 1750.* ☎ *800/ 946-3244 or 787/727-4153. www.at windchimesinn.com. 22 units. Doubles $65–$155. AE, DISC, MC, V. Map p 36.*

★★ **Caribe Hilton** PUERTA DE TIERRA Puerto Rico's first luxury hotel opened in 1949 and still has the power to charm. There's no better place for a piña colada than the Caribe Terrace Bar, which overlooks an infinity pool and the resort's private beach. The resort also has blooming gardens, abuts the historic Fort San Gerónimo, and has a full spa and children's activities. Rooms are larger and more comfortable than most competitors. *Doubles $159–$640. AE, DC, DISC, MC, V. Map p 36.*

★ **kids** **Condado Plaza Hotel & Casino** CONDADO This recently renovated hotel has one of the island's busiest casinos, a lively lobby, several fine restaurants, and plenty for the kids to do. Fresh and saltwater pools overlook a protected beach that is great for toddlers, but there are nicer stretches of sand elsewhere in Condado and Isla Verde. Rooms are big, bright, and airy. *Av. Ashford 999.* ☎ *800/468-8588 or 787/721-1000. www.luxuryresorts. com. 570 units. Doubles $150–$499. AE, DC, DISC, MC, V. Map p 36.*

At Wind Chimes Inn.

★ **kids** **Courtyard by Marriott Isla Verde Beach Resort** ISLA VERDE Out on beautiful and kid-friendly Pine Grove beach by the airport, this renovated property has a wraparound veranda; comfortable, well-furnished rooms; and a quality casino and restaurants. *Av. Boca de Cangrejos 7012.* ☎ *800/791-2553 or 787/791-0404. www.sjcourtyard. com. 293 units. Doubles $160–$385. AE, DC, DISC, MC, V. Map p 36.*

El Canario Inn CONDADO This little bed-and-breakfast, originally built as a private home, is one of the best values along the high-priced Condado strip, right next to the Marriott and close to casinos, nightclubs, and restaurants. It is the best of the El Canario properties. *Av. Ashford 1317.* ☎ *800/533-2649 or 787/722-3861. www.canariohotels.com. 25 units (shower only). Doubles $93–$137. Rates include breakfast. AE, DC, MC, V. Bus: B21 or C10. Map p 36.*

★★ **kids** **El San Juan Hotel & Casino** ISLA VERDE This posh spot still dazzles: from its opulent and consistently entertaining lobby to its setting among century-old

The Gallery Inn.

banyans, verdant gardens, and a golden beach with aquamarine water. The landscaped pool area, restaurants, bars, and nightclub are also tops. The wood-toned Lanias rooms are nicer and more comfortable than the tropical-hued Vista rooms. *Av. Isla Verde 6063.* ☎ *787/791-1000. www.luxuryresorts.com. 382 units. Doubles $192–$1,150. AE, DC, DISC, MC, V. Map p 36.*

★ **Gallery Inn at Galería San Juan** OLD SAN JUAN   From its northern seawall location, this rambling, centuries-old mansion has sweeping sea and cityscape views, verdant courtyards and terraces, an abundance of art and sculpture, and the chatter of tropical birds and the murmur of fountains everywhere one turns. The artist is Jan D'Esopo, who owns the inn with husband Manuco Gandia. The rooftop wine bar and Music Room really add to the inn's appeal. The rooftop terrace has a 360-degree view, an idyllic place to enjoy the breeze or a sunset cocktail. *Calle Norzagaray 204–206.* ☎ *866/572-ARTE or 787/722-1808. www.thegalleryinn.com. 22 units. Doubles $225–$325. Rates include breakfast. AE, DC, MC, V. Bus: Old City Trolley. Map p 35.*

Hosteria del Mar OCEAN PARK This elegant and simple guesthouse is right on San Juan's best beach at Ocean Park. Get an oceanview room; they have either terraces or balconies, tropical decor, comfortable beds, and small but efficient bathrooms. Suites with kitchenettes and apartments are also for rent. *Calle Tapia 1.* ☎ *877/727-3302 or 787/727-3302. hosteria@caribe.net. 27 units. Doubles $69–$239. AE, DC, DISC, MC, V. Bus: A5. Map p 36.*

★★★ **Hotel El Convento** OLD SAN JUAN   This renovated historic beauty offers the quintessential Old San Juan experience and is one of the Caribbean's most charming hotels. Bougainvillea plants bloom against the pastel facades of the centuries-old walls. Its tapas bar, courtyard, and rooftop pool are tops. Rooms are not very big, but they transport one to a luxurious past with Spanish colonial furnishings, four-poster beds, beamed ceilings, paneling, and Andalusian terra-cotta floor tiles. *Calle Cristo 100.* ☎ *800/468-2779. www.elconvento.com. 68 units. Doubles $225–$410. AE, DC, DISC, MC, V. Map p 35.*

Hotel Milano OLD SAN JUAN This 1920s-era hotel has clean, modern facilities at a good price in a great location in SoFo, near some of Puerto Rico's best restaurants and bars along South Fortaleza Street. *Calle Fortaleza 307.* ☎ *877/729-9050. www.hotelmilanopr.com. 30 units. Doubles $85–$185. AE, MC, V. Bus: Old Town Trolley. Map p 35.*

Inter-Continental San Juan Resort & Casino ISLA VERDE The large pool area and boardwalk cafe under the palms and overlooking the beach are its main draws. It just underwent a major renovation that revamped the accommodations and its service philosophy. Standards are finally fulfilling their potential here. *Av. Isla Verde 5961.* ☎ *800/468-9076 or 787/791-6100. www.ichotelsgroup.com. 402 units. Doubles $212–$544. AE, DC, DISC, MC, V. Map p 36.*

★★ La Concha: A Renaissance Resort CONDADO
This tropical modernism landmark was brought back to life 50 years after it opened in December 1958 and instantly became Condado's hottest spot to stay or play. It's famous for its signature seashell restaurant on the beach, and mixes tropical architectural elements like interior patios and exterior blinds to filter the sun's rays toward the building's interior. *Av. Ashford 1077.* ☎ *877/524-7778. www.laconcharesort.com. 248 units. Doubles $199–$439. AE, DC, DISC, MC, V. Map p 36.*

★★ Número Uno Guest House OCEAN PARK
This spruced-up guesthouse looks like it could be in Malibu, but inside you'll find a Spanish courtyard with mosaic tile, gurgling fountains, and pools and beautiful tropical plants. Its restaurant, Pamela's, is one of the city's best (you can eat inside in the dining room or on the beach). There's a variety of luxurious rooms (including apartments), a bar, and a communal terrace. It fronts the best beach in San Juan. *Calle Santa Ana 1.* ☎ *866/726-5010 or 787/726-5010. www.numero1guesthouse.com. 13 units. Doubles $89–$279, apt $169–$279. Rates include breakfast. AE, MC, V. Map p 36.*

★★★ Ritz-Carlton San Juan Spa & Casino ISLA VERDE
Continental elegance and Caribbean style meet comfort and convenience in this top-level resort set on 8 acres (3.2 hectares) of prime beachfront, 5 minutes from the airport. Large, well-furnished rooms have ocean or garden views and top-of-the-line everything. Top-shelf restaurants and bars, as well as San Juan's most upscale casino, round out the amenities. *Av. de los Gobernadores (S.R.) 6961, no. 187.* ☎ *800/241-3333 or 787/253-1700. www.ritzcarlton.com. 416 units. Doubles $285–$769. AE, DC, DISC, MC, V. Map p 36.*

The Ritz-Carlton.

★ San Juan Marriott Resort & Stellaris Casino CONDADO
You won't go wrong staying at this comfortable hotel that is as friendly to families and business travelers as it is to honeymooners. The pool area and beach are among the city's best, and rooms are pretty, large, and comfortable. The lobby and casino are lively (hosting live music nearly nightly). Best of all is its location: in the heart of Condado close to all its restaurants and clubs. The staff is super friendly. *Av. Ashford 1309.* ☎ *800/228-9290 or 787/722-7000. www.marriott.com. 525 units. Doubles $219–$410. AE, DC, DISC, MC, V. Bus: B21. Map p 36.*

Shopping Best Bets

Best **Island Wear**
★★ Hecho a Mano, *Calle San Francisco 260, Old San Juan (p 44)*

Best **Antiques**
★ El Alcazar, *Calle San José, Old San Juan (p 43)*

Best **Puerto Rican Arts & Crafts**
★★ Puerto Rican Arts & Crafts, *Calle Fortaleza 204, Old San Juan (p 46)*

Best **Place to Browse**
★ Bóveda, *209 Calle Cristo, Old San Juan (p 46)*

Best **Local Artists**
★ Galería Botello, *Calle Cristo 208, Old San Juan (p 43)*

Best **Foodie Shop**
★ Spicy Caribbee, *Calle Cristo 154, Old San Juan (p 45)*

Best **for Books**
★ Borders, *Plaza Las Américas, Hato Rey (p 44)*

Best **Jeweler**
★★ Reinhold Jewelers, *Plaza Las Américas, Isla Verde (p 46)*

Best **Shopping Mall**
Plaza Las Américas, *Av. Roosevelt, Hato Rey (p 47)*

Best **Swimwear**
Wet, *Calle Cruz 150, Old San Juan (p 45)*

Cigars at the Cigar House.

Old San Juan Shopping

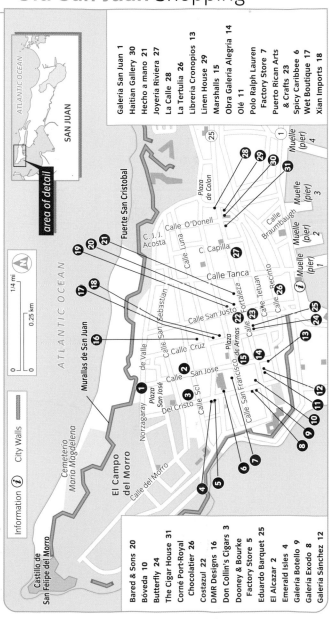

Galeria San Juan 1
Haitian Gallery 30
Hecho a mano 21
Joyeria Riviera 27
La Calle 28
La Tertulia 26
Libreria Cronopios 13
Linen House 29
Marshalls 15
Obra Galeria Alegria 14
Olé 11
Polo Ralph Lauren
Factory Store 7
Puerto Rican Arts
& Crafts 23
Spicy Caribbee 6
Wet Boutique 17
Xian Imports 18

Bared & Sons 20
Bóveda 10
Butterfly 24
The Cigar House 31
Corné Port-Royal
Chocolatier 26
Costazul 22
DMR Designs 16
Don Collin's Cigars 3
Dooney & Bourke
Factory Store 5
Eduardo Barquet 25
El Alcazar 2
Emerald Isles 4
Galeria Botello 9
Galeria Exodo 8
Galeria Sánchez 12

New San Juan Shopping

Belz Factory Outlet World 4
Borders 1
Nono Maldonado 3
Plaza del Mercado de Santurce 2
Plaza Las Américas 1
Reinhold Jewelers 1

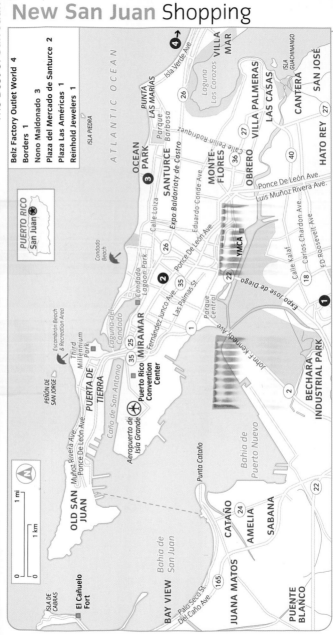

PUERTO RICO
San Juan ★

San Juan Shopping A to Z

Art & Antiques

Butterfly People OLD SAN JUAN
Preserved butterflies from around
the world are displayed in limited-
edition arrangements that will last
forever and can be shipped anywhere. Globetrotting enthusiasts
go gaga for the spot. *Calle Cruz 257.
☎ 787/723-2432. AE, MC, V. Map
p 41.*

★ **El Alcazar** OLD SAN JUAN
Ramble through two buildings full of
antique treasures from throughout
the Caribbean and Europe at the
Caribbean's largest antiques emporium. It stocks everything from Russian icons to turn-of-the-century
Puerto Rican country furniture to silver and ceramics. *Calle San José
103. ☎ 787/723-1229. AE, MC, V.
Map p 41.*

★ **Galería Botello** OLD SAN JUAN
The former residence of Angel
Botello, a Spaniard who made San
Juan his home, is now a showcase
for his paintings and sculpture, as
well as that of many important local
artists. *Calle Cristo 208. ☎ 787/723-
9987. AE, MC, V. Map p 41.*

Galería Exodo OLD SAN JUAN
Young contemporary artists from
the island and across the Caribbean

showcase their work here, which
includes a diversity of styles. *Calle
Cristo 200B. ☎ 787/725-4252. AE,
MC, V. Map p 41.*

★ **Galería Sánchez** OLD SAN
JUAN A new gallery in SoFo that
has assembled a group of talented
international artists with styles ranging from contemporary realism to
neo-impressionist to mixed-media
pop. *Calle Fortaleza 320. ☎ 787/
829-4663 or 787/466-5494. AE, MC,
V. Map p 41.*

Galería San Juan OLD SAN JUAN
This shop sells the sculpture and
paintings of Jan D'Esopo, the Gallery
Inn's resident artist. *In the Gallery
Inn, Calle Norzagaray 204. ☎ 787/
722-1808. AE, MC, V. Map p 41.*

Haitian Gallery OLD SAN JUAN
The bold, bright art of Haiti is the
specialty here: landscapes, crowds,
and jungle animals. *Calle Fortaleza
206. ☎ 787/721-4362. Calle Fortaleza 367: ☎ 787/725-0986. AE,
MC, V. Map p 41.*

Obra Galería Alegria OLD SAN
JUAN A bit off the well-worn gallery route along Calle Cristo and
Calle San José, this gallery is worth
seeking out for its representation of

Santos.

such important masters as Lorenzo Homar, Domingo García, Julio Rosado del Valle, and younger accomplished contemporary artists like Nick Quijano, Jorge Zeno, and Magda Santiago. *Calle Cruz 301 (at Recinto Sur).* ☎ *787/723-3206. AE, MC, V. Map p 41.*

Books

★ **Borders** HATO REY   A huge book, music, and DVD store, plus cafe. *Plaza Las Américas, Av. FD Roosevelt 525.* ☎ *787/767-5202. AE, DISC, MC, V. Map p 42.*

La Tertulia OLD SAN JUAN   A little store with lots of books and music as well as a pretty adjoining cafe. *Recinto Sur 305.* ☎ *787/724-8200. MC, V. Map p 41.*

Libreria Cronopios OLD SAN JUAN   Still known as "the book store," it has a wide selection of books and music (both English and Spanish) in a beautiful Old San Juan setting. *Calle San José 255.* ☎ *787/724-1815. MC, V. Map p 41.*

Carnival Masks

★ **La Calle** OLD SAN JUAN   This shop has the largest selection of brightly painted carnival masks (called *vejigantes*) in San Juan. The

Carnival Masks.

festivals in Ponce and Loíza are among the best spots to see them in action. *Calle Fortaleza 105.* ☎ *787/725-1306. AE, MC, V. Map p 41.*

Cigars

The Cigar House OLD SAN JUAN   This no-frills shop has Puerto Rican cigars and quality Dominican smokes as well. *Inside the Doll House souvenir store, Calle Fortaleza 255.* ☎ *787/723-7797 or 787/725-0652. AE, MC, V. Map p 41.*

Don Collins Cigars OLD SAN JUAN   Hand-rolled on the island with Puerto Rico tobacco or a mix of local and Dominican leaf. *Calle Cristo 59.* ☎ *787/977-2983. AE, MC, V. Map p 41.*

Clothing & Beachwear

Costazul OLD SAN JUAN   This surf shop stocks the latest in beachwear, surf wear, sunglasses, and bathing suits for men, women, and children. The prices are not bad, and the merchandise is top rate—worth a stop if you really need something for the beach. *Calle San Francisco 264.* ☎ *787/722-0991. MC, V. Map p 41.*

★★ **Hecho a Mano** OLD SAN JUAN   Ethnic clothing for women from around the equatorial world, plus handmade jewelry and other accessories. The charming young staff is adorned in it. *Condado & Plaza Las Américas. Calle San Francisco 260.* ☎ *787/722-5322. AE, MC, V. Call for information on the other dozen locations. Map p 41.*

Nono Maldonado CONDADO   The store is named after the owner, a famous Puerto Rican designer and former fashion editor at *Esquire* magazine. They stock upscale ready-to-wear designs for men and women. *Av. Ashford 1051.* ☎ *787/721-0456. AE, MC, V. Bus: A7. Map p 42.*

San Juan Gallery Hopping

Several art galleries have popped up on Avenida de Diego and the area surrounding Calle Canals near the historic **Plaza del Mercado de Santurce (Santurce Marketplace).** But Old San Juan still has the most galleries, selling everything from pre-Columbian artifacts to paintings by well-known local artists like the late, great Rafael Tufiño. Also look for *santos,* the hand-carved wooden saints the island is known for.

Most of Old San Juan's finest art galleries are on Calle Cristo and Calle San José between La Fortaleza and Sol streets. Interesting spots worth a look include **Obra Galería Alegría** (Calle Cruz 301; ☎ 787/723-3206), **Galería Botello** (Calle Cristo 208; ☎ 787/723-9987), and **Galería Exodo** (Calle Cristo 200B; ☎ 787/725-4252). Also take a peek at the **Galería San Juan,** inside the Gallery Inn (Calle Norzagaray 204; ☎ 787/722-1808), featuring the work of Jan D'Esopo, the sprawling Old City mansion's resident artist.

One of the best ways to get a feel for San Juan's vibrant art scene is to attend Noches de Galleria, or **Gallery Nights,** on the first Tuesday of each month. Most galleries have openings or special exhibits, as well as wine-and-cheese receptions, and occasionally live music or theatrical performances. Bars and restaurants get into the act and hold art shows or performances. It all winds up at a party along Calle San Sebastián around midnight.

★★ **Polo Ralph Lauren Factory Store** OLD SAN JUAN   Great prices can be found at this factory outlet, which sprawls through two colonial buildings offering classics from the quintessential American design house. *Calle Cristo 201.* ☎ *787/722-2136. AE, MC, V. Map p 41.*

★ **Wet Boutique** OLD SAN JUAN The personable Erika has owned this shop for decades, selling the hottest swimsuit designs. *Calle Cruz 150.* ☎ *787/722-2052. AE, MC, V. Map p 41.*

Department Stores
Marshalls OLD SAN JUAN   Lots of useful stuff for the traveler at bargain prices: bathing suits, shorts, footwear, luggage, and sunglasses. *Plaza de Armas.* ☎ *787/722-3020. AE, MC, V. Map p 41.*

Food
Corné Port-Royal Chocolatier OLD SAN JUAN   The world's finest Belgian chocolates, pralines, truffles, and other treats. *Calle San Justo 204.* ☎ *787/725-7744. AE, MC, V. Map p 41.*

★ **Spicy Caribbee** OLD SAN JUAN They carry the best selection of gourmet Puerto Rican coffee, such as Alto Grande and Yacuo Selecto, as well as San Juan's biggest and best selection of Caribbean hot and sweet sauces. *Calle Cristo 154.* ☎ *787/725-4690. AE, MC, V. Map p 41.*

Gifts & Handcrafts
★ **Bared & Sons** OLD SAN JUAN One of the most established jewelers in Old San Juan, they sell gold, silver, diamonds, and watches. Insiders head upstairs for the vast

collection of porcelain and crystal—a great source for discontinued patterns at a discount. *San Justo 206 (at Calle Fortaleza).* ☎ *787/724-4811. AE, MC, V. Map p 41.*

★ **Bóveda** OLD SAN JUAN   Exotic jewelry, decor and housewares, clothing, art and cards, and much more is crammed into this great shop. *Calle Cristo 209.* ☎ *787/725-0263. AE, MC, V. Map p 41.*

★ **DMR Designs** OLD SAN JUAN Elegant reproductions and originals of classic Caribbean plantation furniture, more traditional Spanish colonial work, and spare, modern pieces by local artist Diana M. Ramos set this store apart from its competition. *At La Cochera Parking Garage in the heart of the Old City. Calle Luna 204.* ☎ *787/722-4181. AE, MC, V. Map p 41.*

Olé OLD SAN JUAN   The Panama hats, South American silver jewelry, and local *santos* please the crowds here. *Calle Fortaleza 105.* ☎ *787/724-2445. AE, MC, V. Map p 41.*

★★ **Puerto Rican Arts & Crafts** OLD SAN JUAN   Inside a 200-year-old colonial building, the specialty here is high-quality folkloric Puerto Rican art like *vejiantes* (colorful papier-mâché carnival masks from Ponce used to ward off bad vibes), *santos* (wooden statuettes of saints carved by island artisans), and jewelry and clothing inspired by Taino designs. *Calle Fortaleza 204.* ☎ *787/725-5596. AE, MC, V. Map p 41.*

Xian Imports OLD SAN JUAN Island decorators favor this spot as a source for unusual art objects, including Chinese sculptures, paintings, ceramics, and furniture. *Calle de la Cruz 153.* ☎ *787/723-2214. AE, MC, V. Map p 41.*

A woman selling jewelry on Isla Verde Beach.

Jewelry

Eduardo Barquet OLD SAN JUAN   Known as a leading cost-conscious place to buy fine gold, diamonds, and gems, this is one of the Old City's oldest and most renowned stores. *Calle Fortaleza 200 (at Calle La Cruz).* ☎ *787/723-1989. AE, MC, V. Map p 41.*

Emerald Isles OLD SAN JUAN Cost-conscious South American gemstones in silver or gold settings rule the roost here, plus pre-Columbian jewelry reproductions. *Calle Fortaleza 105.* ☎ *787/977-3769. AE, MC, V. Map p 41.*

Joyería Riviera OLD SAN JUAN Another of the Old City's top jewelry stores, this is *the* place for Rolex watches and diamonds. *Calle Fortaleza 257.* ☎ *787/725-4000. AE, MC, V. Map p 41.*

★★ **Reinhold Jewelers** ISLA VERDE   With two locations at the city's top addresses, Reinhold offers creations by internationally renowned jewelry designers and has a David Yurman design boutique. *Plaza Las Américas 24A&B, Hato Rey.* ☎ *787/554-0528. Also in El San Juan Hotel Gallery.* ☎ *787/796-2521. AE, MC, V. Map p 42.*

Shopping Ideas

Puerto Rican arts, crafts, and art objects are well worth buying, including *santos* (wood carvings of the saints by island craftsmen), *vejigantes* (colorful carnival masks), and prints by local artists, usually made for specific events such as festivals. Puerto Rican coffee is the among the world's tastiest, and new gourmet brands like Finca Cialitos are popping up to compete against established premium labels Alto Grande and Yauco Selecto. Puerto Rican rum is also among the world's best. Of course, there's Bacardi, but also quality lesser-known brands like Don Q, an island favorite.

Lace & Linens
Linen House OLD SAN JUAN The spot for *mundillos* (tatted fabrics); the shop's suppliers employ a 500-year-old method of making white lace. Curtains, placemats, tablecloths, and other lovely items are surprisingly affordable. *Calle Fortaleza 250. ☎ 787/721-4219 or 787/725-6233. AE, MC, V. Map p 41.*

Leather
Dooney & Bourke Factory Store OLD SAN JUAN Leather lovers will want to stop here for bargains on buttery handbags and other leather goods. *Calle Cristo 200. ☎ 787/289-0075. Map p 41.*

Malls
Belz Factory Outlet World CANOVANAS This huge outlet mall is just east of San Juan in the shadow of El Yunque rainforest. Stores include Nike, Gap, Dockers, Levi's, Guess, Nautica, and Geoffrey Beene, among others. There are outlet prices for everything, including the cinema. *Hwy. 3 18400, Barrio Pueblo. ☎ 787/256-7040. AE, MC, V. Map p 42.*

★ **Plaza Las Américas** HATO REY The biggest mall in the Caribbean is a remarkable place, even by U.S. standards, with top-name retailers,

full-service restaurants, a Cineplex, two food courts, plus a spa and hairstylists, banks, a post office, and special events from fashion shows to boat shows. *Av. FD Roosevelt 525. ☎ 787/767-5202. AE, MC, V. Map p 42.*

Markets
★ **Plaza del Mercado de Santurce** SANTURCE An old-fashioned Puerto Rican market with stalls and kiosks surrounded by shops, it positively brims with fruit, vegetables, herbs, specialty products, and great local seafood. *Calle Dos Hermanos at Calle Capitol. No credit cards. Map p 42.*

Puerto Rican coffee.

Nightlife & Performing Arts
Best Bets

Best for **Puerto Rican Music**
★★ **Rumba**, *152 Calle San Sebastián, Old San Juan (p 53)*

Best **Dance Floor**
Club Brava, *Hotel El San Juan, 6063 Isla Verde Av., Isla Verde (p 52)*

Best Place to **Drink with Locals**
La Sombrilla de Rosa, *154 Calle San Sebastián, Old San Juan (p 52)*

Best **Music**
Nuyorican Café, *312 Calle San Francisco, Old San Juan (p 53)*

Best **Hotel Lobby**
El San Juan Hotel, *6063 Isla Verde, Av. Isla Verde (p 37)*

Best **Spot for a Sunset Drink**
La Playita, *at La Playa Hotel, 6 Calle Amparao, Isla Verde (p 52)*

San Juan Marriott Resort & Stellaris Casino.

Old San Juan Nightlife

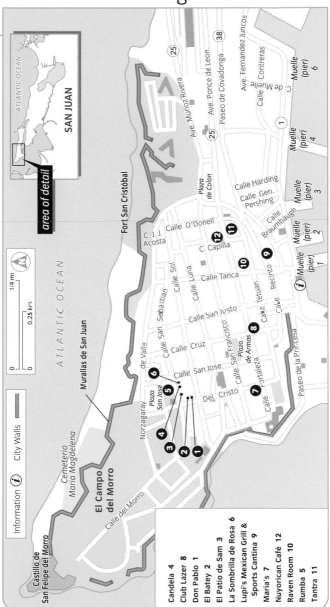

SAN JUAN

ATLANTIC OCEAN

area of detail

ATLANTIC OCEAN

Information ⓘ   City Walls

0   0.25 km
0   1/4 mi

Castillo de San Felipe del Morro

Cementerio María Magdalena

El Campo del Morro

Murallas de San Juan

Calle del Morro

Fort San Cristóbal

Ave. Muñoz Rivera

Ave. Ponce de Leon

Paseo de Covadonga

Ave. Fernandez Juncos

Calle Contreras

C. de Muelle

Muelle (pier) 6

Muelle (pier) 4

Muelle (pier) 3

Muelle (pier) 2

Muelle (pier) 1

Calle Harding

Calle Gen. Pershing

Calle Braumbaugh

Plaza de Colon

C. J. J. Acosta

Calle O'Donell

C. Capilla

Calle Sol

Calle Luna

Calle Tanca

Calle San Sebastián

Calle San Justo

Calle Recinto

Calle Tetuan

Calle San Francisco

Plaza de Armos

Calle Fortaleza

Calle Cruz

Calle San Jose

Calle San José

Del Cristo

Norzagaray

de Valle

Plaza San José

Paseo de la Princesa

ⓘ

Candela 4
Club Lazer 8
Don Pablo 1
El Batey 2
El Patio de Sam 3
La Sombrilla de Rosa 6
Lupi's Mexican Grill & Sports Cantina 9
María's 7
Nuyorican Café 12
Raven Room 10
Rumba 5
Tantra 11

New San Juan Nightlife

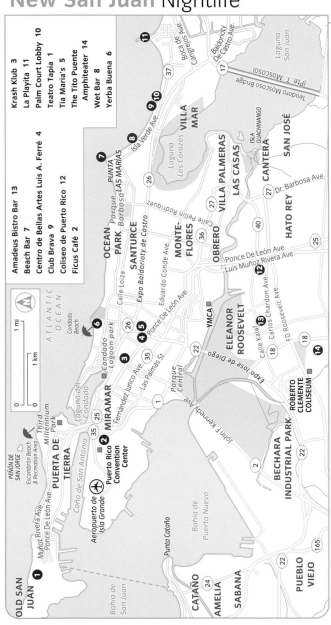

Amadeus Bistro Bar 13
Beach Bar 7
Centro de Bellas Artes Luis A. Ferré 4
Club Brava 9
Coliseo de Puerto Rico 12
Ficus Café 2

Krash Klub 3
La Playita 11
Palm Court Lobby 10
Teatro Tapia 1
Tía María's 5
The Tito Puente
    Amphiteater 14
Wet Bar 8
Yerba Buena 6

San Juan Nightlife A to Z

Performance Venues

Centro de Bellas Artes Luis A. Ferré With several different venues, the Caribbean's best performing-arts center draws exceptional opera, theater productions, and live music performances from the world's finest classical musicians to the top Latin pop stars of the moment. *Av. Ponce de León 22.* ☎ *787/724-4747 or 787/725-7334 for the ticket agent. Tickets $40–$200; 50% discount for seniors. www.cba.gobierno.pr. Map p 50.*

Coliseo de Puerto Rico (The Puerto Rico Coliseum; José Miguel Agrelot) HATO REY Known affectionately as the "Choliseo," this state-of-the-art venue is the island's largest indoor entertainment venue, hosting everything from Rolling Stones concerts and professional basketball games to holiday shows on ice. *500 Calle Arterial B.* ☎ *877/COLISEO (265-4736); ticket office* ☎ *787/294-0001 or 866/994-0001. www.coliseodepuerto rico.com. Map p 50.*

Teatro Tapia OLD SAN JUAN This historic theater on Plaza Colón hosts local, mostly Spanish-language productions, as well as Christmas shows and folkloric events. Call the box office for specific information. *Av. Fortaleza at Plaza Colón.* ☎ *787/721-0180. Tickets $20–$30, depending on the show. Map p 50.*

The Tito Puente Amphitheater (Anfiteatro Tito Puente) HATO REY This charming, more intimate venue inside Hato Rey's Parque Luis Muñoz Marín is the site of the annual Heineken Jazz Fest, one of the world's best venues for Latin jazz, as well as progressive Spanish rock and reggae concerts. *Parque Luis M. Marín, Av. Jesús T. Piñeiro, Esq. Expreso, Luis A. Ferré. Tickets at www.ticketpop.com. Map p 50.*

Pubs, Clubs & Other Spots with Music

Amadeus Bistro Bar HATO REY Live Latin jazz and Spanish ballad singers, and inventive Puerto Rican nouvelle cuisine, make this a winner. Right off the Hato Rey financial district and beside the federal court, it's favored by the local professional

Heineken Jazz Festival.

crowd. *Av. Chardón 350.* ☎ *787/641-7450. Map p 50.*

Candela OLD SAN JUAN   This late-night avant-garde club plays eclectic lounge music into the early morning and hosts experimental music and art events. Cover charges sometimes apply for special events. *100 Calle San Sebastián.* ☎ *787/977-4305. Map p 49.*

Club Brava ISLA VERDE   This club lives up to its surroundings—the elegant El San Juan Hotel lobby—and is a magnet for the young and privileged, local celebs, and urbane visitors. Plan to linger at the bars, cafes, and restaurants surrounding it. Cover is $20. *In El San Juan Hotel & Casino, Av. Isla Verde 6063.* ☎ *787/791-2781. Map p 50.*

Club Lazer OLD SAN JUAN   Right off Plaza de Armas, this is the party spot for cruise-ship workers from around the world when they're in town, plus a young local crowd. Cover is $5. *Calle Cruz 251.* ☎ *787/722-7581. Map p 49.*

Don Pablo OLD SAN JUAN   A battered hole-in-the-wall bar, right next to El Batey, San Juan's original dive throbs to live Spanish pop and avant-garde music as well as the chatter of the local art students who hang here. *Calle Cristo 103. No phone. Map p 49.*

El Batey OLD SAN JUAN   Another dive, its ruined walls are splattered with graffiti and business cards. The conversation is still cut with laughter and irony after all these years—and oh what a jukebox: psychedelic rock, classic Sinatra, and Duke Ellington and Charlie Parker. *Calle Cristo 101. No phone. Map p 49.*

El Patio de Sam OLD SAN JUAN   A bohemian burger joint and late-night fave since the '50s. It offers lively bar banter, often live music, and a nice airy back terrace with great art. *Calle San Sebastián 102.* ☎ *787/723-1149. Map p 49.*

Ficus Café MIRAMAR CONVENTION DISTRICT   Behind this cutting-edge, open-air cafe lies the illuminated Convention Center, the district's centerpiece, while its signature water fountains, a huge dance of liquid and light, front it. The designer food also hits the mark: Don't miss the shark bites or cinnamon chicken croquettes with mango coleslaw. Many special events occur here. *At the Puerto Rico Convention Bureau.* ☎ *787/641-7722. Map p 50.*

La Playita ISLA VERDE   A great bar and restaurant in the back of a small hotel overlooking Isla Verde beach near the Ritz. It's a great spot for a quiet drink at night or a break from the beach during the day. It serves breakfast through dinner. *At Hotel La Playa, 6 Calle Amapola.* ☎ *787/791-7298. Map p 50.*

La Sombrilla de Rosa OLD SAN JUAN   Great neighborhood bar with daily specials and weekday lunches with great *comida criolla* at prices ranging from $5.50 to $7.95. Sporadic live entertainment on some nights. It has the best bargains on beer in the Old City. *Calle San Sebastián 154. Map p 49.*

Lupi's Mexican Grill & Sports Cantina OLD SAN JUAN & ISLA VERDE   The live *rock en español* is as hot as the tacos, fajitas, and burritos served here, plus some tasty basic pub fare. Yankees fans take note: The owner is former ace Ed Figueroa. *Isla Verde: Av. Isla Verde, Km 187;* ☎ *787/253-1664. Old San Juan: Recinto Sur 313;* ☎ *787/722-1874. Map p 49.*

Maria's OLD SAN JUAN   Reliably mixed blender drinks served at a bar with history. Ignore the food and tacky decor. *Calle Cristo 204.*

A salsa band.

☎ 787/721-1678. Bus: Old City Trolley. Map p 49.

Nono's OLD SAN JUAN The bar overlooks the action on Plaza San José while the jukebox blares. *47 Calle Cristo.* ☎ 787/579-5851.

Nuyorican Café OLD SAN JUAN Last time they were in town, Mick Jagger and Keith Richards came straight here for the salsa. You should too. This hotspot also has Latin jazz, reggae, Spanish rock, and other performances. They serve great pizza, too, until 1am. *Calle San Francisco 312 (entrance down the alley).* ☎ 787/977-1276 or 787/366 5074. Map p 49.

Palm Court Lobby ISLA VERDE One of the Caribbean's most beautiful, the mahogany and marble oval-shaped bar is set in a sunken area beneath a huge, glittering chandelier. It's a choice spot to glimpse the good life: well-heeled travelers, local celebrities, and the young and beautiful. *In El San Juan Hotel & Casino, Av. Isla Verde 6063.* ☎ 787/791-1000. Bus: A5. Map p 50.

Raven Room OLD SAN JUAN Trance and house music in a shamelessly trendy "club lounge" that's too luxurious for its own good. It

doesn't really get going until after midnight. *Recinto Sur 305.* ☎ 787/977-1083. Map p 49.

★★ **Rumba** OLD SAN JUAN A great venue for salsa, Latin jazz, and other Caribbean music, and to watch the locals so gracefully gyrating to it on the big dance floor in front of the stage. Another mustsee. *Calle San Sebastián 152.* ☎ 787/725-4407. Map p 49.

★ **Tantra** OLD SAN JUAN A custom martini menu and the best latenight menu in town. The decor and cuisine are a heavenly mix of the best of Indian and Puerto Rican influences. *Calle Fortaleza 356.* ☎ 787/977-8141. Map p 49.

Wet Bar ISLA VERDE On the 11th floor of a boutique hotel, this bar looms over the Atlantic coastline and is a perfect spot for watching the sun set. It's all R&B romance and swooning jazz, with comfy furnishings and sushi under the stars completing the vibe. *In The Water Club, Calle José M. Tartak 2.* ☎ 787/728-3666. Map p 50.

★★ **Yerba Buena** CONDADO Tasty Cuban food accompanies live salsa, Latin Jazz, and bohemian music several nights a week. *Av. Ashford 1350.* ☎ 787/721-7500. Map p 50.

Dancing the Rumba.

Hitting the Casinos

Most San Juan hotels have casinos, and there are also large casinos at some of the bigger resorts outside the city. Most are casual, but they don't allow swimsuits or shorts. Hours are noon through 4am.

The 8,500-square-foot (790 sq. m) casino at the **Ritz-Carlton** (Av. de los Gobernadores, Isla Verde; ☎ 787/253-1700) is the largest in Puerto Rico. It features traditional games such as blackjack, roulette, baccarat, craps, and slot machines.

One of the splashiest of San Juan's casinos is at the **Old San Juan Hotel & Casino** (Calle Brumbaugh 100; ☎ 787/721-5100), where five-card stud competes with some 240 slot machines and roulette tables. But the busiest game room in town is probably the **Condado Plaza Hotel & Casino** (Av. Ashford 999; ☎ 787/721-1000), which also benefits from several great restaurants. **El San Juan Hotel & Casino** (Av. Isla Verde 6063; ☎ 787/791-1000) also has a great gaming room, right off its grand lobby, still one of San Juan's top nightspots. **The San Juan Marriott Resort & Stellaris Casino** also has a lively scene, especially on weekend nights (1309 Ashford Av.; ☎ 787/722-7000). Of the resorts outside San Juan, the most striking is the casino at El Conquistador, a circular disk at the island's northeast corner, with windows all around looking out over the sea and the undeveloped coastline surrounding the resort. James Bond film fans will recognize it from *Goldfinger.*

Gay & Lesbian

Beach Bar CONDADO This bar is on the back deck of Condado's most popular gay hotel, fronting its most popular gay beach, with the party really starting to get going around 4pm. *Atlantic Beach Hotel, Calle Vendig 1.* ☎ *787/721-6900. Map p 50.*

Krash Klub SANTURCE This multilevel club has a mixed clientele with a shared party attitude. It could be in downtown New York or L.A. Gorgeous dancers, cutting-edge music, beautiful bars, and plush bathrooms. Cover is $20. *Av. Ponce de León 1257.* ☎ *787/722-1131. Map p 50.*

Tia Maria's Liquor Store SANTURCE This bar attracts men and women, a mostly gay and lesbian crowd. It's right around the corner from the Puerto Rico Art Museum and the Centro de Bellas Artes, not to mention near several fine restaurants. *Av. José de Diego 326 (near the corner of Av. Ponce de León).* ☎ *787/724-4011. Map p 50.* ●

3 The Best Full-Day Tours

The Best **in Three Days**

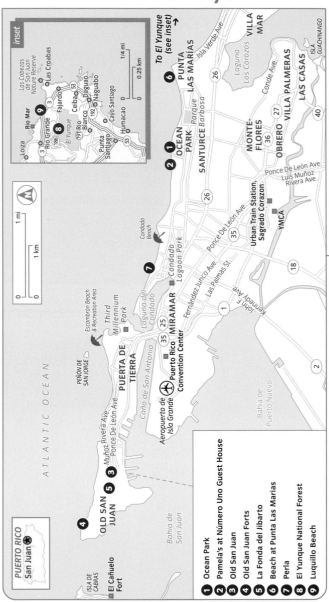

Previous page: La Muralla.

1 Ocean Park
2 Pamela's at Número Uno Guest House
3 Old San Juan
4 Old San Juan Forts
5 La Fonda del Jíbarto
6 Beach at Punta Las Marías
7 Perla
8 El Yunque National Forest
9 Luquillo Beach

Puerto Rico is large when compared to most Caribbean islands. If you have only 3 days, concentrate on San Juan, which has fine beaches, cultural and historic sights, the Caribbean's finest nightlife, and perhaps its most vibrant culinary scene. The depth of Puerto Rican visual arts and musical performance, local architecture, and cuisine is astounding at first exposure—and the appreciation only grows with time. There is ample evidence of this in San Juan, and the breadth and sophistication of the city is surprising—everything from a performance by Russian soprano Anna Netrebko to the first-rate Puerto Rico Philharmonic Orchestra might be happening on any given night. But Puerto Rico's dirty secret might be that its biggest city, San Juan, has some of its finest beaches. Even better, most major sites in Puerto Rico can be experienced on leisurely day trips from the capital.

Most visitors prefer a hotel or guesthouse by the beach, but if shopping, nightlife, and culture are more your style, consider one of Old San Juan's fine lodging options. This tour has you based out of San Juan for 2 nights, with a full day trip out on the island. You'll be able to see some of the best attractions Puerto Rico has to offer and will have the greatest variety of experiences with this game plan.

From the airport, the closest beach district is Isla Verde, followed by Ocean Park and then Condado. They range from about 2 to 6½ miles (3–10km) from the airport to Old San Juan. Take a flight arriving in San Juan as early as possible on Day 1 so you can spend most of the day after check-in at the beach or at the hotel pool. If you want to stay at a big hotel with a large pool, the best bet is either Isla Verde or Condado, which have some of the best beaches and finest properties on the island.

1 ★ **Ocean Park.** I prefer the low-key experience of Ocean Park. The beach is beautiful and so is the crowd: an interesting mix of urbane visitors, students, young professionals, and active families. Take it all in at Calle Santa Ana, where you can partake in a little paddleball or just watch the kite-surfers whiz by. The water is great for swimming in the summer and bodysurfing in the winter. You can luxuriate in the sun for

several hours, ensuring your trip gets off to the right start, and still have time for other pursuits before sunset.

Low-key Ocean Park.

Travel Tip

For detailed descriptions of the beaches in this chapter, see chapter 6. For hotel reviews and more on recommended restaurants, see chapter 2. For more on watersports and other activities, see chapter 7.

2 ★ **Pamela's** at Número Uno Guest House has teak tables and chairs beneath the palms right on the beach. If you can get beyond the smooth, chilly fruit frappes and tropical cocktails, the pan-Caribbean cuisine and snacks are top notch. See more in chapter 2. *At Número Uno Guest House, Calle Santa Ana 1.* ☎ *787/726-5010. Main courses $15–$35. AE, MC, V. Lunch and dinner daily. Bus: A5. Map p 32.*

Break from the beach in early afternoon, showering and changing at your hotel, so that you can head into Old San Juan for a bit of

sightseeing or shopping and a great meal. Budget-minded travelers can take an A5 or B53 bus for 75¢, but you'll have to cab back home if you make a night of it.

3 **Old San Juan.** Old San Juan is one of the best neighborhoods in the Caribbean; with so much to see, you'll likely return more than once, even during a 3-day trip. This afternoon's goal is to take in a few sights and begin soaking up its atmosphere, as you work up an appetite for dinner. Walk along the southern edge of charming Plaza Colón, Calle Fortaleza, to enter the historic district. This area is called SoFo and is

Old San Juan.

packed with some of the island's best restaurants, tonight's dining destination. But first browse through the artisan shops and art galleries, retail factory outlets, and clothing boutiques along the block. For a complete walking tour of Old San Juan, see p 10.

4 Old San Juan Forts. Most visitors will want to return to the Old City in the morning, if only to explore the twin, historic Spanish fortresses, **El Morro** (p 20) and **San Cristóbal Fortress** (p 19), and perhaps see the **Museo de las Américas** (p 23), near El Morro. From Plaza Colón, walk north up the hill along Calle Norzagaray to enter the San Cristóbal Fortress. El Morro is at the other end of town, along the ocean-side boulevard, on a anvil-shaped headland overlooking the entrance to San Juan Bay. Art and antiques lovers will want to spend some time rummaging through shops and exploring the city's many fine galleries, whereas history buffs will find treasures of their own in the many museums and historic sites, and shoppers will find a vibrant bazaar of shops and artisans selling their wares streetside.

Excellent fishing lies off San Juan's coast.

For more information on Old San Juan, see chapter 2.

5 Have a hearty lunch of *cocina criolla* before leaving the Old City, either at **La Fonda del Jibarito** (p 31) or **Raices** (p 33), where you're sure to get a heaping helping of local culture along with the

Getting Around San Juan

The public transportation might not be on par with New York or Boston, but it is a lot cheaper and more highly developed by Caribbean standards. Buses serve most of the city from 5:30am to 11:30pm every day. There's also an 11-mile (18km) light-rail system (called Tren Urbano) as well as plentiful taxicabs and public cars, which charge flat rates for longer trips and take on several passengers.

While Puerto Rico is legendary for its traffic jams and the spirited style of many local drivers, the truth is it probably has the most advanced roadway system in the Caribbean, and renting a car is the way to go if you want to tour outside San Juan. If you stay in the city, go by public transport or cab, depending on your budget.

Travel Tip

For detailed descriptions of transportation options, see "Getting Around" on p 163.

faultless renditions of classic dishes, from stuffed *mofongo* to chicken and rice. See chapter 2.

6 Outdoor recreation. Return to the beach if **tanning and relaxation** is your goal. Alternatively, you can easily take **kite-surfing, windsurfing, surfing, or scuba lessons** or rentals in San Juan, or even arrange for a half-day **deep-sea fishing** charter. Today is the day most golfers will want to cut out for a game. See chapter 7.

7 Nightlife. Make it a point tonight to enjoy some of the nightlife of the capital, bar-hopping, taking in the club or music scene, or going casino gambling. Condado

has been undergoing something of a redevelopment revival, so dine at its heart at **Perla** (p 32), the fabulous seashell-shaped restaurant on the beach at La Concha Hotel, a tropical modern beauty that was restored on its 50th birthday in December 2007. You're likely to find La Concha's lobby a great spot to tap the pulse of the city's nightlife after the meal. The lobby's sleek interior facades and furnishing blends are joined by fountains and small pools to layered landscaped exteriors, where drinks and tapas are served under the stars. Like any San Juan hotel worth its salt, La Concha has an adjacent casino and nightclub.

Luquillo Beach with El Yunque in the background.

Luquillo Beach food stall.

From the airport, take Baldorioty de Castro Expressway (PR 26) to the Roberto Sánchez Vilella Expressway (PR 66), which brings drivers to Canóvanas, along the eastbound lane of Hwy. 3. At Palmer, turn right to turn onto Rte. 191. Follow signs to El Yunque along to more lefts and the turn right onto Rte. 9938, which climbs into the verdant nature reserve.

8 ★★ El Yunque National Forest. The 28,000-acre (11,331-hectare) El Yunque Forest is the only tropical rainforest in the U.S. National Forest Service system. **El Portal Tropical Forest Center** (Rte. 191; ☎ 787/888-1880; daily 9am–5pm; $3, $1.50 for children under 12) has maps and guidance, but maneuvering through the park can be done through signs posted along the main road. Most of its best attractions can be seen on only a short hike of no more than 3 hours. See p 141.

From the El Yunque, exit at Palmer, go east along Rte. 3, and follow signs for Balneario de Luquillo. Turn left at Calle Fernández García. Take a left on Rte. 193, which leads to the entrance at the right.

9 Luquillo Beach. Have lunch at one of the many fine seafood restaurants in the kiosks beside the Luquillo Public Beach. You'll see them on your left side along Rte. 3, just before the exit to the public beach, which is where you access these modest restaurants. **La Roca Taína,** No. 60, at the far eastern end of the kiosk area, is the closest to the public beach. It has plenty of options, from barbecued chicken to fried red snapper to mofongo stuffed with Caribbean lobster, and conch and codfish ceviche. It gets a little rowdy on weekends, with a fun beach party vibe and a loud jukebox, but so does everywhere in Puerto Rico.

10 Spend the rest of your day at the beach before heading back to San Juan. The public beach has snacks, drinks, restrooms, showers, and changing facilities. Downtown Luquillo is located at the exit to Rte. 992.

The Best **in One Week**

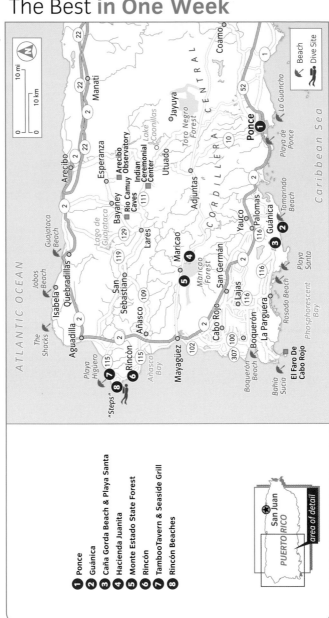

1 Ponce
2 Guánica
3 Caña Gorda Beach & Playa Santa
4 Hacienda Juanita
5 Monte Estado State Forest
6 Rincón
7 TambooTavern & Seaside Grill
8 Rincón Beaches

|deally, I recommend you stay at least a week on Puerto Rico to take in this vibrant, multifaceted island at a pace slow enough to enjoy its charms. This weeklong itinerary adds a few favorites to the 3-day tour: A trip to Ponce and the southwest coast, a stop in a mountain town, and then the northwest coast. **START: From San Juan, drive south along the Luis A. Ferré Expressway, then Highway 2 west to Ponce.**

Parque de Bombas.

It's 75 miles (121km) southwest to the city of Ponce—via Las Américas Expressway and then Hwy. 52, the Luis A. Ferré Expressway. You'll take it over the spine of the Cordillera Central mountain range, and down onto its Caribbean coastline, traversing west to Ponce along Rte. 2.

① Budget about 2 hours to see downtown Ponce—more if you plan to lunch there. You'll want to visit ★ **Plaza Las Delicias,** with its historic **Lion Statue Fountain,** and **Parque de Bombas** (p 89), a black-and-red Victorian wooden firehouse. Several more historic structures are nearby. The **Museo de Arte de Ponce** (p 92), with a stunning collection of European classics, as well as broad holdings

of local and regional artists, will reopen in 2010 after a 2-year renovation. Also of interest are El Vigia watchtower and adjacent attractions and La Guancha public boardwalk and marina, with harborfront restaurants, frequent entertainment, and a ferry to an offshore island. There are a few fine restaurants in downtown Ponce and in the La Guancha area (including the nearby Ponce Hilton resort). Or stop by Las Cucharas on your way out of town, a string of restaurants overlooking a peaceful Caribbean cove offering fresh seafood and *comida criolla.* One of the most renowned is **La Montserrate, Las Cuchara** (Rte. 2; ☎ 787/841-2740; entrees $12–$26; AE, DISC, MC, V; lunch and dinner daily).

Guánica Dry Forest.

Continue west along Hwy. 2 until Rte. 116, which takes you to the beach towns of Guánica, La Parguera, and Boquerón.

2 Guánica. The three main lodging options in this town are among the best in their class in the region, and Guánica has the most and the most varied beaches. It's still a bit off the beaten tourist path, but has some fine seafood restaurants as well as world-class amenities, including the restaurant at the Copamarina Beach Resort. Budget some time to explore the town's Dry Forest, which extends to the coastline. It can be reached from the road extending beyond Copamarina through an undeveloped stretch of coastal land astounding in its beauty.

3 ★ Cana Gorda public beach & Playa Santa. The town's best beaches are the Cana Gorda public beach, next to Copamarina, and Playa Santa, beyond Barrio Ensenada, which housed what was once the Caribbean's largest sugar mill, and still bears the mark of its colonial past through the American-style plantation architecture left standing. You'll have several hours on your first day and several hours

the next day to enjoy the sun. For lodging details, see chapter 5.

Head west along Hwy. 2 to Sabana Grande, where you will take Rte. 120 up into the mountains at Maricao. Once in town, take Rte. 119 to the hotel. You'll need to head west by 3pm—an hour or 2 earlier if you plan to stop in San Germán—in order to make it to your mountain lodging by nightfall (which I recommend doing).

4 Hacienda Juanita. This beautiful mountain inn with a restaurant lies in the coffee country of Maricao, a lush world still uncorrupted by modern development. There's also a fine restaurant at the parador. *See p 112.*

5 Get up early and explore the **Monte Estado State Forest**, with its chilled pools fed by mountain streams. You'll want to head out early, however, to arrive in **Rincón,** more than an hour away.

The best way to drive is through a maze of roads from the inn, starting with Rte. 119 and right on Rte. 4406, and continuing on this road until you intersect with Rte. 108. Follow Rte. 108 until you intersect with Rte. 406. Take that road to Rte 109 (Calle 65 de Infanteria), which you will take until Rte 115, where you will turn left. Follow Camino Carrertas through the tourist district.

6 Rincón is a gorgeous town surrounded by sea and wide, fine-grained white beaches, which sprawl across a blunt highland jutting out from the island's west coast. There's no finer sunset in the Caribbean. Long a surfer's paradise with a few decent guesthouses, it is now one of Puerto Rico's biggest draws for visitors. Lodging options range from quality economical choices to luxury getaways for the finest tastes and biggest wallets. Ditto for dining options. Apart from beautiful beaches, Rincón has world-class surfing, great deep-sea fishing, scuba, snorkeling, and sailing opportunities. For more on Rincón, see chapter 5.

7 Have a sunset drink or snack (or full meal—the fresh seafood is excellent) at the **Tamboo Tavern**

and Seaside Grill Restaurant, which has a back deck and dining tables among the sand dunes and palm trees brimming with a beautiful crowd. *Carr. 413 Km 4, Sandy Beach.* ☎ *888/823-8550. Entrees $16–$26. AE, MC, V. Lunch & dinner Thurs–Tues.*

8 Beach time in Rincón. Hopefully, you're flying out late, so you can enjoy several hours of beach time on Rincón before having to fly back home. (Check about the availability of return flights from Aguadilla, which will extend your beach time by at least 2 hours.) The Aguadilla airport is 17 miles (27km) north on the former Ramey Air Force Base.

From Rincón, take Rte. 4402 to Hwy. 2, which you take north. Take the Rafael Hernández Airport/Punta Borinquen exit at Hwy. 7. Take a left at Calle San Rafael and then onto Rte. 107, which you will take until Av. Borinquen. Bear right at the ramp and then turn right onto Av. Ing Orland Alarcon, which leads to the airport entrance.

Surfing in Rincón.

The Best in Two Weeks

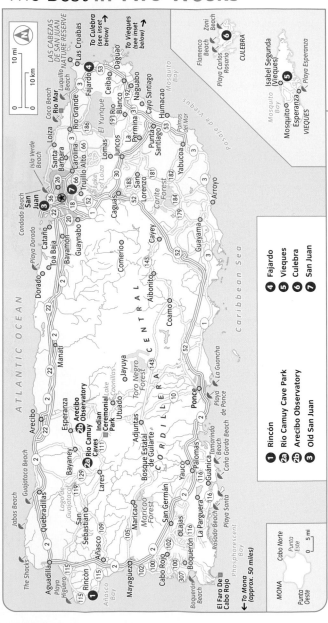

1 Rincón
2A Río Camuy Cave Park
2B Arecibo Observatory
3 Old San Juan
4 Fajardo
5 Vieques
6 Culebra
7 San Juan

Two weeks will allow you to explore all that Puerto Rico has to offer, rolling several different vacation experiences into one. You can spend enough time to thoroughly immerse yourself in San Juan and have enough time to visit an array of picture-perfect beaches, which extend from Culebra off the east coast to Rincón in the west. After you've had enough sun, you can head to the central mountains to chill out and relax in the quiet tropical countryside. You should add this week-long itinerary to the "The Best in One Week," itinerary earlier in this chapter. START: **Rincón.**

① Rincón. Spend an extra night in Rincón, which will allow you to really enjoy its charms.

The observatory can be reached heading west on Hwy. 22 and then taking Rte. 10 south, the start of a 20-mile (32km) roller-coaster journey. Take exit 75B and go right on Rte. 652, and then left on Rte. 651. Go straight at the intersection of Rtes. 651 and 635 and then turn left at the cemetery onto Rte. 625, which will lead you to the entrance to the observatory. The Rio Camuy Cave Park is south of Arecibo, at Km 18.9 along Rte. 129, the road to Lares.

② ★ Rio Camuy Cave Park and/or Arecibo Observatory. Head back toward San Juan early with the idea of taking in at least one of the two major attractions en route—the Rio Camuy Cave Park (p 145) or the Arecibo Observatory (p 105). It's possible to see both and get back to San Juan in the early evening. You'll need 2 hours to visit the caves, and an hour and a half for the observatory.

Take Hwy. 116 to Hwy. 2, which leads to Expressway 53 Rte. back to Old San Juan.

Río Camuy Cave Park.

③ Stay in **Old San Juan** for a different kind of experience. Walk from your hotel and have a great meal, then stroll around the various nightspots, following the music you enjoy listening to. You won't be spending any time at the beach this time. You're arriving late and leaving early.

Follow directions to El Yunque; then take Hwy. 3 into Fajardo. At Avenida Valero, turn left. Turn left again at Calle A Norte and then right at Calle D. Take Avenida El Conquistador beyond the resort to Avenida Cabezas, which passes the Fajardo's Seven Seas Public Beach before entering the Las Croabas fishing village. The town harbor is near both lodging options and is the base for snorkeling, kayaking, and many sailing trips in the area.

④ Fajardo. Your next destination is Fajardo, and there are only two places to stay: the budget-conscious and pleasant **Fajardo Inn**, or the expansive and elegant **El Conquistador Resort and Country Club** (p 117).

Definitely plan a few hours at the beach and go to **Seven Seas Public Beach** (35 miles/56km east of San Juan), where a 2-mile (3km) hike through a trail in

Vieques.

the shrub forest on its eastern end leads to ★ **El Convento Beach,** a miles-long stretch of largely untouched beachfront, home to sea turtles and reef-studded waters with great snorkeling. The official vacation home of Puerto Rico's governor is the only development to speak of. The dirt road leading to it is the only road near the beach, one of the reasons it has been able to escape the stampede of development that has remade most of Puerto Rico.

⑤ Vieques (p 119). You can take a ferry from Fajardo or take a flight from San Juan or Ceiba. For those who know Puerto Rico, this island often seems like a microcosm of the bigger island, frozen in time in an unspecified past, with patches of rolling pasture land, gnarled hills, and dirt roads, and with a mix of rough Atlantic and tranquil Caribbean coastline. For decades, the U.S. Navy controlled two-thirds of the island, which was perhaps the most resonant evidence of Puerto Rico's century-long colonial relationship with the United States. But the Navy left in 2003, and the town has

been doing better ever since as it gradually gets control of more land, builds better lodgings and restaurants, and receives increasing international notice. There are 40 gorgeous beaches. Yeah—40.

⑥ Culebra (p 129). You might have to take a ferry back to Fajardo, but it's still probably the best way to go. Let the tropical decompression continue and sail off to this neighboring island, which is smaller, quieter, and more low-key and underappreciated than Vieques. It's still a small place, but there are many top-notch lodging and dining options.

⑦ San Juan. Return to San Juan, which will start to feel like home about now, to relive a special moment, or to get another chance to experience all you want to in the capital city. The flight from Culebra is hassle-free and a mere half-hour. Return to that great guesthouse you stayed in at the start of your trip, or splurge on a night at El Convento.

⑧ Get your last licks at shopping or the beach before jetting out of the airport. ●

Puerto Rico **with Kids**

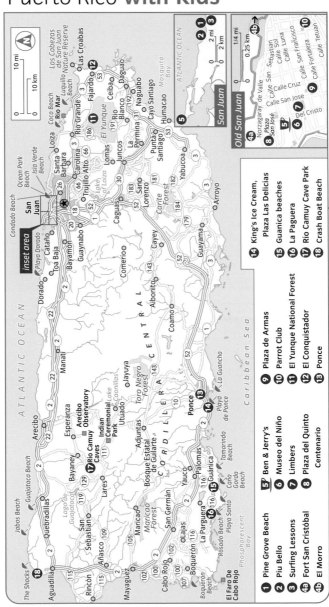

San Juan

Old San Juan

1. Pine Grove Beach
2. Piu Bello
3. Surfing Lessons
4a. Fort San Cristóbal
4b. El Morro
5. Ben & Jerry's
6. Museo del Niño
7. Limbers
8. Plaza del Quinto Centenario
9. Plaza de Armas
10. Parrot Club
11. El Yunque National Forest
12. El Conquistador
13. Ponce
14. King's Ice Cream, Plaza Las Delicias
15. Guanica beaches
16. La Paguera
17. Rio Camuy Cave Park
18. Crash Boat Beach

Previous page: Cerro Gordo Beach.

Puerto Ricans love children, so you'll feel super-welcome with your kids, be they colicky infants or rowdy preteens. Travel can make kids groggy and cranky, hyped up, or just plain moody, so be ready to adjust your schedule and don't plan to do too much. But Puerto Rico has much to enchant children of all ages. Kids can run through ancient forts, learn to surf, or take a ferry to the Bacardi rum distillery for a free tour—and so can you. The 7-day itinerary below covers the major clusters of family activities available in Puerto Rico, but you'll likely find still more activities and places that would appeal to your family in the tours and other information that follow. Let's face it: Kids, especially if they are escaping winter, want to be in the water, whether it's the ocean or the hotel pool, or taking advantage of the many other activities available to them at major hotels in San Juan and throughout Puerto Rico. For this reason, this tour leaves plenty of time for fun in the sun and the other childhood activities pursued at leisure. START: **San Juan. Length: 7 days.**

❶ Spend the day enjoying your hotel's amenities. If you are staying in a large property, there's probably a kids' activity center onsite, with organized watersports, arts and crafts, as well as other activities for children. Most pools also keep kids entertained, but check for extras, like the Marriott's waterslide, which is a big hit. San Juan has wide, inviting beaches, but the best beach for families is Isla Verde's Pine Grove Beach, especially its western end fronting the Ritz-Carlton. The other option is the Marriott Courtyard Isla Verde, at the other end of the beach. The beach connects to the Carolina Public Beach, which is an option for those who stay elsewhere; it has the same tranquil surf as well as showers, changing facilities, restrooms, and other facilities. Condado's surf can get rough in winter, which you should keep in mind if your kids prefer the ocean over a hotel pool. The little beach outside the entrance to the Condado Lagoon, beside the Condado Plaza Hotel, is protected and is always calm.

Enjoying the San Juan Marriott Resort's kid-friendly pools.

2 You might want to explore the area for dinner (see family-friendly restaurants below) and then get dessert at one of several ice-cream shops running throughout the city's tourist districts, from Old San Juan through Isla Verde. All the big chains are here, but a local favorite is **Piu Bello,** which serves up excellent Italian-style ice cream and tasty light meals, including breakfasts, wraps, and salads. *At the Hotel Coral by the Sea, 2 Calle Rosa, Isla Verde.* ☎ *787/791-9945. Sun–Thurs 8am–11pm, Fri & Sat 8am–1pm.*

3 **Surfing lessons.** Start off the next day giving your kid something he won't forget: surfing lessons, right on Isla Verde's Pine Grove Beach. There are a few surf pros right between the two hotels offering lessons, foam board included. William Sue-A-Quan tore up the pro circuit for a decade and now teaches kids ages 6 to 70. Most learn to stand up and ride waves during the first lesson. He's right on the beach a block east of the Ritz-Carlton (Walking On Water Surfing School; ☎ 787/955-6059; www.gosurfpr.com). You can also arrange for parasail rides and other watersports activities behind Isla Verde's main beach behind Isla Verde Avenue, right near El San Juan Hotel and Casino.

Learning to surf.

Museo del Niño.

If you book the surfing lesson at 8am, you can grab a quick snack and take a cab to the forts in Old San Juan before noon, another must-see for the kids. From Plaza Colón, walk up the hill at Avenida Norzagaray to get to the entrance of Fort San Cristóbal.

4 **Fort San Cristóbal and El Morro.** Make sure to show the kids the walls of the dungeon, which are still marked with the drawings of ships etched by prisoners and the remote Devil's Sentry Tower, a lookout over a dramatic point of crashing waves and rock. A single admission is good for the city's two fortresses. El Morro holds even more fascinating opportunities for children of all ages to amble through its tunnels, ramps, vaults, and dramatic lookout points from lonely watchtowers and gunnery posts.

5 **Ben & Jerry's.** Grab a wrap or sandwich and have an ice cream. It's a great spot for the kids to hang out with music, Internet, magazines, and so on. The ice cream is delicious, with the cones cooked up on the spot. *61 Calle Cristo.* ☎ *787/977-6882.*

⑥ The Museo del Niño (Children's Museum). This museum will keep toddlers entertained the entire afternoon, but kids older than 7 will find an hour or so of entertainment, mostly in and around the rooftop science and nature exhibits. There's a children's play area, a theater with shows, simple human body exhibits, and an arts and crafts area. There's also a padded play area for kids under 3 and a mock village complete with a market. *150 Calle Cristo. Admission $5 adults, $4 children 14 & under.* ☎ *787/722-3791. Tues–Thurs 9am–3:30pm, Fri 9am–5pm, Sat–Sun 12:30–5pm.*

Walk down the alley between the museum and the Hotel El Convento. On the right, beyond the Caleta Guesthouse, right across from Plaza Rogativa, is a little sign that says LIMBERS.

⑦ Limbers. A local family has sold tasty frozen tropical ices from this window for generations. Be sure to share this San Juan tradition with your family.

Walk up the shaded roadway closest to the bay. It's an alternate route to El Morro, and a lovely walk past the lush garden of the historic home of Juan Ponce de León and a park.

Flying kites on the grounds of El Morro.

⑧ Once the sun has gone down a bit, in the late afternoon and early evening, skateboarders practice their moves to island urban rhythms outside the adjacent historic Spanish military barracks on **Plaza del Quinto Centenario** and children fly kites on the massive grounds of **El Morro.** Don't worry if you don't have one; you can buy a cheap kite from the street vendors selling snacks on the border of the grounds to the fortress, which is set back against a flattened green bluff.

From El Morro, go back toward Plaza San José and walk east along Calle San Sebastián, known for its bars and nightlife. Take a right down Calle Cristo, which cuts through the heart of the city, Plaza de Armas, the home of City Hall and the State Department, to Calle Fortaleza.

⑨ Plaza de Armas. At the center of Old San Juan, this is a good place to stop by so your kids can buy feed and heave it at the flocks of pigeons. There are two outdoor cafes on the plaza and ice-cream shops.

⑩ A family meal. Try **Raíces** (p 33) for some authentic *comida criolla* in an ambience that pays homage to Puerto Rico's folkloric

Stay Here!

If you can afford it, stay at El Conquistador, the mammoth resort on a bluff, with a tram down to its bayside marina level, a ferry to its private island, and a new water park for the kids. If you're on a budget, the nearby **Fajardo Inn** offers an attractive experience, with its own Coco's Water Park, a collection of slides and fountains in the area of the children's pool.

The elusive Puerto Rican Parrot.

arts; or the bright, tropical **Parrot Club** (p 32) for contemporary takes on Latin classics.

Take Baldorioty de Castro Expressway (PR 26) to the Roberto Sánchez Vilella Expressway (PR 66), which intersects with Hwy. 3 at Canóvanas. Head east until Palmer; then turn right onto Rte. 191 and then Rte. 9938 as you climb into the verdant 28,000-acre (11,200-hectare) rainforest.

⑪ Drive to El Yunque National Forest, the only tropical rainforest under federal jurisdiction, 32 miles

El Yunque pathway.

(52km) east of San Juan. **El Portal Tropical Forest Center** (Rte. 191; ☎ 787/888-1880; Daily 9am–5pm; $3, $1.50 for children under 12) is educational for kids, but skip it if your time is limited. Hiking trails and other points of interest are signposted. The Forest Center has maps and guidance for visitors, but maneuvering through the park can be done through signs posted along the main road. Most of its best attractions can be seen with only short hiking in a morning visit of not more than 3 hours. See p 141 for more details.

Show the kids La Coco Falls and the watchtower lookout, both along the main road. Take the hike to La Mina Falls for a swim in the cold-water pond at its base. With the falls crashing down from above, and green jungle surrounding them, it's the perfect spot for a break.

Continue east to your destination, Fajardo—the town on the northeast coast of Puerto Rico that has much to fascinate the family. No matter where you stay, follow signs for El Conquistador Resort & Golden Door Spa and Las Croabas, the charming fishing village that the sprawling resort

The pools at El Conquistador.

towers over. Take Rte. 987 past the resort's entrance and then the Seven Seas public beach and Las Cabesas de San Juan nature resort to the small harbor, where a string of seafood restaurants and food vendors surrounds the square that fronts it. It's a great spot for a cheap, filling lunch of local fare.

⑫ Enjoy your digs. Especially if you stay at El Conquistador, you'll need the entire day to enjoy the facilities: a regular pool, water park, marina and private island for the beach, and a tramway and ferry to take you everywhere. You'll need a full day just to take it all in. If you are not staying there, you might want to fit in an afternoon at the Seven Seas public beach, a beautiful arc of sand in front of a gentle beach, conducive to building sandcastles, playing water volleyball, tossing the Frisbee, or engaging in a surf-line paddle-ball competition. The main event of the day for most, however, is falling back into the salty surf, usually with a drink in hand.

Leave early the next day for Ponce, heading south along the coastal Hwy. 3 rather than the PR 53 Expressway. This way, you can pass through peaceful fishing towns like Naguabo, which has a harbor filled with open-air seafood restaurants and a remarkable Victorian mansion, before heading south to what once was sugar country, Humacao and Guayama. Around Yabucoa and Maunabo, take Rte. 901, a mountain roadway screaming down to breathtaking coastline. It connects again with Hwy. 3, which passes through more sugar country. Beyond Guayama, you will exit Hwy. 3 to head west along Hwy. 2, which hugs the island's south coast, passing through Ponce. Here, you'll pass through banana plantations and rolling cattle pastures.

⑬ Ponce. Kids love the Victorian firehouse and the huge monuments and fountains on Plaza las Delicias. There is also a wide variety of lunch spots for all tastes and budgets (see chapter 5). A free town trolley goes throughout the historic zone and also takes passengers on a loop around other attractions of interest, principally La Guancha, the town's boardwalk-marina area where there's always something going on, the El Vigia lookout, and the Serrallés Castle overlooking town.

Ponce's Victorian firehouse.

14 King's Ice Cream (right across from the firehouse; 9322 Calle Marina; ☎ 787/843-8520) is a Ponce institution, serving up homemade tropical ice cream for a half-century. Many of the flavors—like tamarind, passion fruit, and soursop—might be new for visitors.

Don't hang around Ponce too long; if you hurry, you can take a swim at fantastic beaches in Guánica during the afternoon and make it to your destination at La Parguera for check-in and dinner, then an after-dinner cruise through a glowing bay.

La Parguera.

Continue on Hwy. 2 outside Ponce as it winds along the Las Cucharas sector. You'll drive through mostly rural and suburban coastland until Yauco, a former coffee-growing center that extends from the steaming coasts through the central mountains. Just beyond the exit is the so-called Porta del Sol, Rte. 116, which passes through one of Puerto Rico's most welcoming coastlines, with over two dozen beaches spread between Guánica and Cabo Rojo.

Once you reach Guánica, take the exit for Rte. 333, which climbs above the town's main harbor to a beautiful coastal bluff overlooking the huge bay. The road zigzags through hilltops of dry forest and surges down along mangrove-lined coastline. You'll drive past the Caña Gorda public beach, then the beautiful Copamarina Beach Resort and beyond it, through a wild, beautiful, undeveloped landscape, where the town's dry forest tumbles down to undeveloped coastline.

15 There are about a dozen different spots to **stop for a swim** along the route above. Alternatively, you could take a short boat ride to a small island with beaches and mangroves just offshore. See chapter 6.

Afterwards, head west along Hwy. 116. You'll drive past the beautiful Lajas Valley, virgin farmland extending up into the central highlands in the distance, before turning off at the La Paguera exit.

16 La Parguera. This peaceful coastal town has some good restaurants and lively bars and is an excellent sailing and scuba center. After checking in and having dinner (see chapter 5 for information), you should still have time for a boat ride to the town's phosphorescent bay in a glass-bottomed boat. *See p 147.*

Wake up early for the drive to Aguadilla along Hwy. 2, about an hour north. Past Mayagüez, it passes atop a cliff overlooking the impressive coastline. Your destination is the Marriott Courtyard Aguadilla (p 107), which caters to families and is close to some of the northwest's best beaches. Head northeast on Rte. 304 and take it until Hwy. 116,

where you will turn left to the west. Head 1.2 miles (2km) to Rte. 101 and then travel 2.4 miles (3.9km) to Calle Comerio Luna, where you will turn right and then turn left on Rte. 122. Next, take a right at the Mayagüez Hwy. 2 signs, and then head for the Hwy. 2R/Aguadilla downtown exit. Turn right on Hwy. 2R, then left at Calle José Pinero. The hotel is on your right side.

17 Río Camuy Cave Park. Spend an hour or so at the pool and then take the kids for a drive to the nearby Río Camuy Cave Park, a beautiful place of gorgeous caverns, underground rivers, and a wild natural landscape of Caribbean forest and limestone foothills. If your children are science buffs, you might consider skipping the pool or the cave park and visiting the Arecibo Observatory instead. *See p 145.*

18 Crash Boat Beach. Spend your last day on the beach, one of the prettiest and most convenient for families. If the kids are looking for something different, remember that there's also a water park in town. *See p 136.*

Exploring a cave in Karst country.

Relax & Rejuvenate
in Puerto Rico

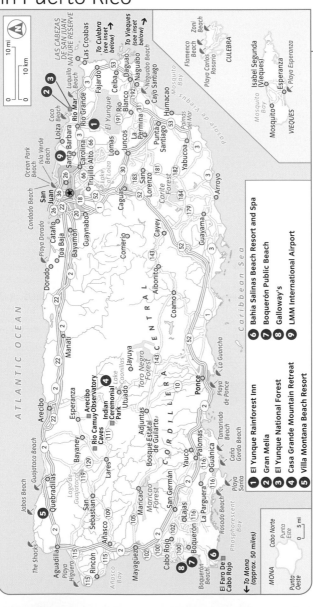

1. El Yunque Rainforest Inn
2. Gran Melia
3. El Yunque National Forest
4. Casa Grande Mountain Retreat
5. Villa Montana Beach Resort
6. Bahia Salinas Beach Resort and Spa
7. Boquerón Public Beach
8. Galloway's
9. LMM International Airport

Island resorts have all upgraded their spa facilities and services in recent years, making it easier than ever to rest and relax during your vacation. Visitors can also find rejuvenation by leaving behind the large coastal resorts and exploring the inns of lush coffee country and rainforest, which cater to visitors looking to unwind and get away from it all. START: **El Yunque Rainforest Inn, Length: 5 days.**

From the airport, head east on Expressway Baldorioty de Castro (PR 26) and take it to Expressway Roberto Sánchez Vilella (PR 66), which takes you to Canóvanas on Hwy 3. Take it east, toward Fajardo and Río Grande. Take the exit for Rte. 956, which is before the Palmer exit that you take for the forest reserve. After the exit at Rte. 956, follow signs for Galateo. Turn right on Rte. 186. The inn is on your right.

❶ **El Yunque Rainforest Inn** is a low-key virgin rainforest retreat just 45 minutes from the airport. The Villa, $165 per night, has an elegant lodge feel (complete with a fireplace) and is the nicer of the two offerings for couples. The management also offers a $500 villa that sleeps four and up and has a pool. The inn serves healthy breakfasts and has a great library with books and movies, a Wi-Fi connection, and a house computer. You'll breathe in fresh air and really relax. The Lost Machete Trail is a challenging hike through the Inn's 5-acre

(2 hectare) rainforest plot, descending down along a jungle stream to a beautiful waterfall. This is private property in the midst of the federal rainforest reserve, so you will likely encounter very few people, if anyone at all. There are also massage and other spa services. El Yunque Caribbean National Forest surrounds the property, so you are at a perfect vantage point to explore. Take the Lost Machete Trail on your first afternoon. *See p 117.*

Head to Hwy 3 and turn left to the west and follow signs for the resort. Exit to the right at Calle B, which will have a large sign for the resort, and then another right at Calle A. Take one more right at the unmarked Calle No. 15.

❷ For dinner on your first night, drive to the swanky **Gran Melia** (p 117) to splurge on gourmet local food in a relaxed setting, at Pasion or one of the resort's excellent Asian or Italian restaurants.

Enjoying a massage at the Intercontinental San Juan.

A trail in El Yunque.

❸ Wake up early and explore the **El Yunque National Forest.** *See p 141.*

Head back toward San Juan and continue west beyond it by picking up PR 22 (the De Diego Expwy.). You can make it to Casa Grande by 1pm if you leave by 11am. At Arecibo, exit at 75B to take PR Hwy 10 to Utuado and Adjuntas. Exit to the left on Rte. 111. Stay on Rte. 111, exiting to the right onto Avenida Herrera. Turn left at Calle Catano, which is also known as Rte. 612.

❹ **Casa Grande Mountain Retreat.** Head to this former coffee plantation set on 100 acres (40 hectares) of lush tropical forest, with yoga, massage, hiking trails, and a freshwater pool. The thing to do here is just kick back and do nothing—a real stress-busting experience. *See p 112.*

This is the Caribbean, after all, so head down to the coast. Return to Arecibo, heading west on Expressway De Diego (PR 22) until it ends. Merge into Hwy 2. At Isabela, exit on Rte. 113. Turn right at Calle Emilio González and right again on the Municipal Hwy Road, Carretera Municipal. Then turn left on Rte. 466 to:

❺ **Villa Montana Beach Resort** (p 107). Villa Montana is an upscale but eco-friendly Caribbean plantation-style resort with 50 separate villas, each with its own veranda. It has 3 miles (4.8km) of beach and plentiful amenities. You can have the quintessential Caribbean experience of horseback riding on the beach here. Isabela is one of the most beautiful towns along Puerto Rico's hundreds of miles of coastline. Make sure to drive along Rte. 466 exploring the beaches and sinkholes, and the rustic

Horseback riding at Villa Montana Beach Resort.

Walking a deserted beach.

eateries and quaint guesthouses that mark the area. See chapter 5.

Go south long Hwy 2 as it hugs the west coast above Mayagüez and descends along the peaceful southwestern region. Take exit 161 to Rte. 100 toward Cabo Rojo. Take this to Rte. 301, then 3301. At Calle Tamarindo, turn left, then turn left again on the next unmarked road, which takes you to the property.

⑥ Spend your last night on the island on its sleepy southwest corner, a dramatic landscape of rocky coastline, salt flats, stunted forests, and beautiful beaches. The windswept area surrounding the Cabo Rojo lighthouse has the serene yet desolate feel of the Maine coast, but made over for the tropics. The **Bahia Salinas Beach Resort and Spa** (p 96) is nearby, a surprisingly stylish, full-service property surrounded by a wildlife reserve and undeveloped coastline.

From the resort, take Rte. 3301 to Rte. 301 until it intersects with Rte. 101, also called Calle Betances. Take a left on Rte. 101 and travel about a mile (1.6km). Right before entering the village of Boquerón, you'll have to bear left to stay on

Rte. 101, which leads to the entrance of the public beach.

⑦ Make sure to visit the beautiful **Boquerón Public Beach** nearby, one of Puerto Rico's finest, with so much room you can find secluded spots on the busiest of holiday weekends. Likewise, you should visit the village of Boquerón, with modest yet lively bars, restaurants, and guesthouses. *See p 136.*

From the beach, drive back to Rte. 101, then turn left to head into the village of Boquerón.

⑧ **Galloway's,** in town, is one of the most relaxing ways to wind down a day. Sit in the back dining room, which is on a deck right over the water, and watch the sunset, the Caribbean spreading out endlessly in every direction. *See p 96.*

⑨ You'll probably fly home from San Juan today. It's a beautiful drive. You'll pass the sweeping Lajas Valley, verdant flatlands stretching out to the distant hills, and then the south-coast highway all the way to Salinas, where you will begin your ascent over the central mountains and back down the other side, a slow descent back to the city and your ultimate destination.

Romantic Puerto Rico

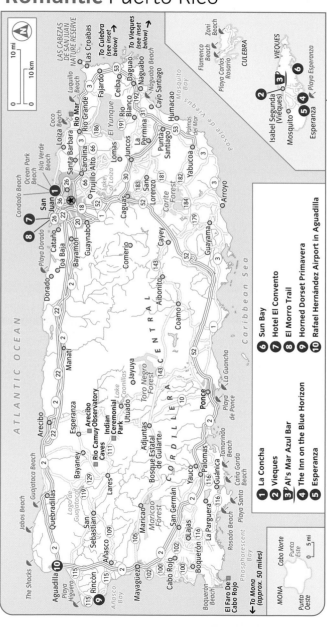

1 La Concha
2 Vieques
3 Al's Mar Azul Bar
4 The Inn on the Blue Horizon
5 Esperanza
6 Sun Bay
7 Hotel El Convento
8 El Morro Trail
9 Horned Dorset Primavera
10 Rafael Hernández Airport in Aguadilla

Lovers will swoon over Puerto Rico, which pulsates to sensuous rhythms and is enveloped with the scent and feel of the tropics, regardless of where you wander. Whether you are looking for a romantic dinner and a night of dancing, have your heart set on finding a secluded hideaway with a view all to yourselves, or want to get pampered at a world-class resort, you'll be able to enjoy it on Puerto Rico together. START: **La Concha, Av. Ashford 1077, Condado, San Juan.**

La Perla is a modernist gem of a restaurant.

❶ You'll both feel sexier with a tan, so stay at **La Concha** (p 39), San Juan's most fashionable beach hotel, just 15 minutes from the airport, on your first day. The infinity pool fronts a splendid stretch of beach, and the oceanfront rooms spill into the blue horizon.

The lobby at this modern tropical jewel, which underwent a $320-million renovation to celebrate its 50th birthday, is all cutting-edge urban cool seamlessly stitched with natural splendor: lush plants, gushing waterfalls, a multilevel pool area, and the beach beyond. Two of San Juan's finest restaurants are steps away: Perla (p 32), the hotel's seashell-shaped restaurant that sits right on the beach; and Budatai (p 30), the deliciously situated and plush Nuevo Latino-Asian emporium of Puerto Rico's "Iron Chef" Roberto Treviño. No matter how far you stray from the hotel, you won't find comparable flavor and atmosphere. There's no place better for a nightcap than at La Concha's lobby, where you can mingle with the beautiful crowd at the bar or enjoy a drink on one of the peaceful terraces surrounding the open lobby.

❷ **Vieques.** An hour after leaving La Concha, you can be in Vieques, an unvarnished tropical island that looks like a smaller version of the main island of Puerto Rico, but 50 years ago. Take a cab to the nearby

Isla Grande airport for the 20-minute flight. Arrange to have your rental jeep meet you at the airport. Drive along the dreamy country roads of Vieques on your way to the Inn on the Blue Horizon. Take Rte. 200, which hugs the north coast, east to head into the main town of Isabel Segunda, with sleepy, shady plazas; unvarnished wooden homes; and stone businesses of genuine architectural character.

3 Stop for a drink and snack in town and soak up some local flavor. **Al's Mar Azul Bar** (p 123), right beside the ferry dock, attracts an eclectic crowd at all hours, and the view of Vieques Sound to the mainland is priceless. Several nearby vendors and small bars sell fried seafood turnovers and other local delicacies. Be sure to try the chilled conch ceviche salad, a local specialty.

Head back out of town as if going toward the airport along Rte. 200, but turn south at the intersection with Rte. 201, which cuts through the rolling heartland

of this beautiful island. Where it intersects with Rte. 996, right before arriving at the village of Esperanza, is the Tienda Verde, which is your best bet for food or supplies. Esperanza is a charming coastal village with a row of simple guesthouses and restaurants fronting the harbor. You'll continue through it and continue up the road to arrive at your destinations.

4 **The Inn on the Blue Horizon** (p 127) sits on an oceanfront bluff and is the most reliable recommendation for couples on a romantic holiday. You'll probably spend most of the day lounging by the pool and beach. Make a point to tour the island's few main roads sometime before sundown to both get a feel for your surroundings and appreciate how beautiful they are. The inn's Blue Moon Bar is one of the best spots on the island to have a drink and watch the sunset.

5 Grab **breakfast in Esperanza** (the Trade Winds [p 127] is famous for its hearty and fresh fare) and then go exploring, in search of a secluded beach.

Sunset on Vieques.

The pool at the Inn on the Blue Horizon.

Take Rte. 996 east and then take the cutoff for Rte. 997. Farther along the road beyond Sun Bay lies the entrance to the Vieques National Wildlife Refuge, a former Navy base that hosts some of the island's most beautiful beaches, such as Red, Blue, and Plata.

6 Sun Bay. Spend the day at a beautiful public beach. The entrance to Sun Bay also gives access to Media Luna and Navio (p 137), where visitors can sometimes find privacy.

Afterward, head back west along Rte. 996 beyond Esperanza for a tour of Vieques's rural center. Take Rte. 201 north and then pick up Rte. 995 through the hills around Pilón. The area looks completely undeveloped, but there are gorgeous vacation homes in the hills above the woods. Pick up the north-coast Rte. 200 near the airport; but if you have time before your flight, you should drive west to Green Beach. You'll drive through a beautiful nature reserve and eerie reminders of its military past, with acres of munitions bunkers rippling through the land.

7 If you catch a flight by 4pm to Isla Grande, you'll have time to check in at the gorgeous **Hotel El Convento** (p 38) in Old San Juan and take a leisurely stroll around Cristo and La Fortaleza streets to see the shops and sites before a restful cocktail at the hotel overlooking its gorgeous interior courtyard. Your room has Spanish colonial furnishings, high-beamed ceilings, large four-poster beds, and fine linen. An intimate splash pool and

Walking along El Morro's walls.

The Horned Dorset's pool.

sun deck are on the roof. There are plenty of spots for a romantic dinner and maybe a little Latin Jazz afterward. For more information on dining and shopping, see chapter 2.

8 An evening promenade.
El Morro Trail provides scenic views along San Juan Bay as it runs along its coast from the San Juan Gate out around El Morro, to the desolate base of the huge fortress's seawall, a point called the Bastion de Santa Barbara. The walk passes El Morro's well-preserved walls. The walkway was designed to follow the undulating movement of the ocean, and sea grapes and tropical vegetation surround benches. The trail is romantic at night, when the walls of the fortress are lit up.

9 You'll want to linger a bit in the morning, but after a leisurely

breakfast, you'll have a long drive to the **Horned Dorset Primavera** (p 106) in the west-coast town of Rincón. The secluded boutique resort sprawls across 8 acres (3.2 hectares) of isolated beachfront and lush gardens. Constructed on the breakwaters of a century-old railroad, flowers bloom everywhere in this hacienda-style resort. The well-appointed rooms are plush retreats with private plunge pools, sun decks, or interior terraces. With a fine restaurant on the premises, and each other, there's absolutely no reason to go anywhere for at least 2 days.

10 If you planned well, you'll have an early evening flight so you can stretch your stay as long as possible. Fly home from the Rafael Hernández Airport in Aguadilla, a 30-minute drive to the north. ●

5

The Best **Regional & Town Tours**

Ponce & the Southwest

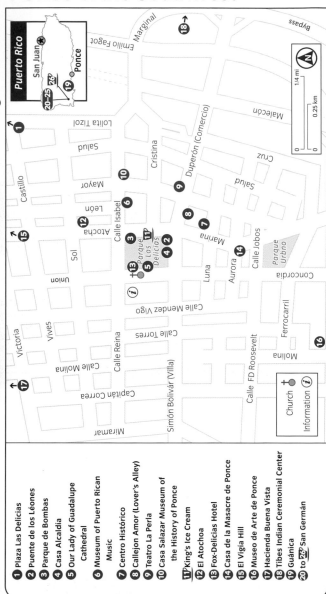

Puerto Rico

San Juan

Ponce

1 Plaza Las Delicias
2 Puente de los Léones
3 Parque de Bombas
4 Casa Alcaldia
5 Our Lady of Guadalupe Cathedral
6 Museum of Puerto Rican Music
7 Centro Historico
8 Callejon Amor (Lover's Alley)
9 Teatro La Perla
10 Casa Salazar Museum of the History of Ponce
11 King's Ice Cream
12 El Atochoa
13 Fox-Delicias Hotel
14 Casa de la Masacre de Ponce
15 El Vigia Hill
16 Museo de Arte de Ponce
17 Hacienda Buena Vista
18 Tibes Indian Ceremonial Center
19 Guánica
20 to 25 San Germán

Church
Information

Previous page: Parque de Bombas detail.

"The Pearl of the South" is stuck in the past, a provincial Spanish colonial town where life passes by slowly, men wear guayaberas, and uniformed schoolchildren fill the plaza with laughter on hot afternoons. Most visitors go to Ponce to see the city's renovated historic section. Although the city dates back to 1692, its unique "Ponce Creole" architecture—mixing Spanish colonial, neoclassical, Caribbean, and contemporary influences—dates from the 1850s. It melds continental style with the tropical climate and was created during Ponce's heyday as a regional trading power, which brought foreign influences not only to its architecture, but also to other aspects of its culture, such as food, music, and art.

There are more than 1,000 historic buildings in Ponce, and most have been restored. The major points of interest are on streets surrounding Plaza Las Delicias (Plaza of Delights). START: **Plaza Las Delicias.**

❶ ★ Plaza Las Delicias. This beautiful central plaza, with wide mosaic-tile walkways, leafy trees, and groomed gardens, is lined with trimmed Indian laurel trees and turn–of–the century lampposts.

❷ Puente de los Léones. The plaza is home to one of the most beautiful fountains in Puerto Rico, Puente de los Léones, or Lion Fountain, a marble and bronze

monument constructed for the 1939 World's Fair that now stands guard over the historic city.

❸ ★ Parque de Bombas. Also on the plaza is the black-and-red Parque de Bombas, an 1882 wooden Victorian firehouse whose facade is synonymous with the city itself. *Plaza Las Delicias.* ☎ 787/284-3338. *Free admission. Daily 8am–5pm.*

Parque de Bombas.

Casa Alcaldía (City Hall), Ponce.

④ Casa Alcaldía (City Hall). On the plaza's south side is Casa Alcaldía, built in 1840. It is marked by its clock tower, imported from London in 1877, and a monument to American troops killed in the Spanish-American War.

⑤ Our Lady of Guadalupe Cathedral. The plaza is also home to Our Lady of Guadalupe Cathedral, known for its alabaster altars and huge pipe organ. *Calle Concordia/Calle Union.* ☎ *787/842-0134. Free admission. Mon–Fri 6am–12:30pm; Sat–Sun 6am–noon & 3–8pm.*

Our Lady of Guadalupe Cathedral.

Walk to the northern border of Plaza Las Delicias and go right to Calle Isabel to get to:

⑥ Museum of Puerto Rican Music. Inside one of the city's most beautiful and intricately detailed private residences, the museum showcases the Indian, Spanish, and African roots of island music. Displays include instruments, music memorabilia, and information on composers and performers. *Calle Isabel 50.* ☎ *787/848-7016. Free admission. Wed–Sun 8:30am–4:30pm.*

Walk down to the Plaza Las Delicias's southeast corner and continue along Calle Marina 1 block to:

⑦ Centro Histórico. This reception center was built in 1922 and now hosts government agencies.

⑧ At the corner of Marina and Duperón are **two historic bank buildings,** marked by stained-glass widows, Art Nouveau details, and other unique features. The banks are separated by a narrow alleyway, lined with African tulip trees. It is called Callejon Amor, or **Lover's Alley.**

From the plaza's Calle Marina border, take Calle Cristina west 1 block to see:

9 Teatro La Perla. Off the plaza along Calle Mayor is this renovated neoclassical building built in 1864 and known for its stellar acoustics. It's the largest historic theater in the Spanish Caribbean. The lobby is often left open for rehearsals during the day and it's sometimes possible to sneak a peek inside. During late afternoons it's also possible to listen to singers or musicians rehearsing. Everything from plays to concerts is held here. *At Calle Mayor & Calle Cristina.* ☎ *787/843-4322.*

Take Calle Mayor 1 block north to Calle Isabel, where you will find:

10 Casa Salazar. The Moorish-inspired Casa Salazar is among the city's most charming architectural treasures. Built in 1911, with neo-classic and Moorish details, the residence also deploys typical Ponce Creole style: stained-glass windows, mosaics, pressed-tin ceilings, fixed jalousies, wood and iron columns, porch balconies, interior patios, and the use of doors as windows. Today it hosts the **Museum of the History of Ponce,** which traces this town's story back to the time of the Tainos. *Calle Isabel 51–53 (at Calle Mayor).* ☎ *787/844-7071. Free admission. Tues–Sun 9am–5pm.*

11 King's Ice Cream (☎ 787/843-8520), right across the street from the Parque de Bombas on the city's main square, has been scooping up delicious ice cream for decades. Another option for a drink or sandwich is the **Café Tomas/Café Tompy** (Calle Isabel at Calle Mayor; ☎ 787/840-1965).

Walk north of the plaza 1 block along Calle Marina. At Calle Sol you will find:

12 El Atochoa. North of Plaza Las Delicias is the city's marketplace district, a group of streets made into a pedestrian area. This is the spot to go for local color and some real bargains.

13 On the plaza's western edge is the **Fox-Delicias Hotel,** a pink-walled Art Deco beauty built in 1931 as a movie house. It's a good spot for a drink.

Walk 2 blocks south from Plaza Las Delicias along Calle Marina. At the Corner of Calle Aurora you will find:

14 Casa de la Masacre de Ponce. Also near the plaza is this museum located at the site of a March 21, 1937, Nationalist Party protest march that turned violent, with police killing 19, including women, children, and innocent bystanders, and wounding 100. The confrontation took place right outside the former shoemaker's shop that houses the museum. It provides a concise, unvarnished history of the modern independence movement and the official repression often brought against it. *Corner of calles Aurora & Marina.* ☎ *787/844-9722. Free admission. Daily 8am–noon.*

The Art Deco facade of Fox-Delicias Hotel.

Museo de Arte de Ponce.

A free trolley operates from Plaza Las Delicias, connecting downtown Ponce with other tourist attractions. Take it to El Vigía Hill.

⑮ El Vigía Hill. The city's tallest geologic feature (300 ft./91m) dominates Ponce's northern skyline. Its base and steep slopes are covered with a maze of 19th- and early-20th-century development. At the summit, the Cruz del Vigía (Virgin's Cross) rises 100 feet (30m) high and measures 70 feet (21m) across. There's an observation tower serviced by an elevator within the structure. There's also a Japanese botanical garden with bonsai plantings and elevated bridges running between ponds and streams—a perfect spot to relax. The gardens surround **El Museo Castillo Serrallés,** an Andalusian-style castle built during the 1930s by the rum-making Serrallés family. Walk through the huge courtyards to enjoy the panoramic views. *El Vigía 17.* ☎ *787/259-1774. Admission $9 adults, $4.50 seniors, $4 children & students (includes all attractions on El Vigía Hill). Tues–Sun 9:30am–5pm. Free trolley leaving from Plaza Las Delicias de Ponce. Take Ruta Norte. (northern route) 9am–9pm every day.*

⑯ ★ The trolley also brings you to **Museo de Arte de Ponce** (closed for renovations until 2010). Founded by former Gov. Luis A. Ferré, the founder of today's pro-statehood New Progressive Party, the museum has the finest collection of European and Latin American art in the Caribbean. Its most iconic piece may be Fredrick Lord Leighton's *Flaming June.* The building itself is a beauty, with unique curved stairways in the open lobby and a hexagonal layout designed by Edward Durell Stone. *Av. de Las Américas 23–25.* ☎ *787/848-0505. www.museoarteponce.org.*

To the north of Ponce are some fine, easily accessible attractions in the rural mountains overlooking the city.

From Avenida de las Américas, it's a 20-minute drive to the first attraction. Head west down the avenue until the intersection with Rte. 500, which you will take to Rte. 123 (Calle La Poncena) and turn left. At Km 16.8 you will find:

⑰ Hacienda Buena Vista, which is located in Barrio Magüeyes along the rural mountain road to Adjuntas. This restored coffee plantation, originally constructed in 1833, shows visitors what life was like on an island farm more than a century ago, with furnishings from the time period, as well as methods of agricultural production, with working water wheels on site. *Rte. 123 Km 16.8, Barrio Magüeyes.* ☎ *787/722-5882 (daily); 787/284-7020 (weekends). Tours $7 adults, $4 children & seniors. Reservations required. 2-hr. tours Wed–Sun at 8:30 & 10:30am and 1:30 & 3:30pm (in English only at 1:30pm).*

To get to the next attraction, head east along Av. Las Américas, turning left at Av. De Hostos, which turns immediately into Calle Salud. You will then take a left at Calle Trioche and a right at Calle Mayor Cantera. This road turns into the Carretera Tibes, which you will follow to Rte. 503, where you turn right. You will then bear left to stay on this road, which leads to:

18 Just north of Ponce, the **Tibes Indian Ceremonial Center** has the oldest pre-Columbian burial ground discovered in the Antilles, dating from A.D. 300. It has ancient pre-Taíno plazas, seven huge rectangular ball courts, and dance grounds marked by stone formations lined up with celestial events. *Rte. 503, Tibes, at Km 2.2.* ☎ *787/ 840-2255. Admission $3 adults, $2 children. Guided tours in English & Spanish are conducted through the grounds. Tues–Sun 9am–4pm. 2 miles (3.2km) north of Ponce.*

Take Hwy. 2 west of Ponce to Rte. 116 for:

19 The beach district encompassing **Guánica, La Parguera, Boquerón,** and other area vacation communities like El Combate. You can easily while away 3 fine days exploring different beaches, taking boat rides offshore, and exploring

natural areas like the **Guánica Dry Forest** and the **Cabo Rojo Lighthouse.** See p 145 and 147.

Continue straight on Hwy. 2 to get to San Germán, Puerto Rico's second-oldest town and a cultural treasure.

20 ★★ **San Germán** dates to 1512 and has been home to pirates, escaped slaves, French conquerors, and renegade Spanish, a legacy today's residents wear proudly. Its historic downtown, like Old San Juan, has Spanish colonial, Creole, Art Deco, and other architectural restorations. There are some 249 restored historic houses listed in the city, but few are ever open to the public. They are all clustered together, uphill from Calle Luna, the sector's main thoroughfare.

21 ★ **Iglesia Porta Coeli (Gate of Heaven).** On the crest of a hill overlooking the Parque de Santo Domingo, this church was built in 1606, making it the oldest in the New World. Constructed in the Romanesque style borrowed from northern Spain, it has a tough palm-wood and ausubo-beam ceiling and its exterior is sheathed in smooth salmon-colored stucco. It has an astonishing *santos* collection, a

Historic building, San Germán.

Casa Morales, San Germán.

17th-century portrait of St. Nicholas de Bari, the French Santa Claus, and a 19th-century statue of Señora de la Monserrate, the Black Madonna. *Corner of Calle Ramos & Calle Santiago Vevé, Plazuela Santo Domingo, San Germán.* ☎ *787/892-0160. Admission $3 adults, $2 seniors & children over 12, free for children under 12. Wed–Sun 8:30am–noon & 1–4:30pm.*

㉒ **Casa Morales.** Just downhill from Iglesia Porta Coeli is the Casa Morales, a wooden Victorian mansion with wraparound porches, circular rooms, and peaked tower ceilings.

㉓ **Parque de Santo Domingo.** The plaza fronting the church is a former marketplace lined with cast-iron benches and busts of prominent figures in the town's history.

㉔ This plaza merges gracefully with a second, the **Plaza Francisco Mariano Quiñones,** or the **Plaza Principal,** which is home to the old **City Hall** and the impressive **San Germán de Auxerre.** First built in 1573, but substantially reconstructed after that for more than a century, the baroque cathedral has a gorgeous trompe l'oeil ceiling, a huge rock-crystal chandelier, and 10 altars and three chapels. ☎ *787/892-1027. Daily 8–11am & 1–3pm.*

㉕ The entire downtown is lined with scores of **beautiful historic buildings,** some exquisitely

Getting Around

The town's inner core is small enough that everything can be visited on foot. Taxis provide the second-best alternative. There is a free trolley connecting the historic zone with the La Guancha harbor area, the Ponce Hilton, and the El Vigía area tourism attractions. Maps and information can be found at the tourist office, Paseo del Sur Plaza, Suite 3 (☎ 787/841-8044). It's open daily 8am to 4:30pm.

restored, others in desperate need of repair. Bougainvillea spills from balconies while lush gardens and mosaic tile line interior courtyards like in Andalusia.

Walk east along Santiago Vevé 2 blocks to:

26 Tapas Café. This cool dining room, with mosaic tiles and blue stars, is a welcome respite from Old San Germán's hot streets. Try the sangria and the large, classic tapas and Spanish classics like Caldo Gallego and paella a la marinara. *50 Calle Dr. Santiago Vevé, San Germán.* ☎ *787/264-0610. Tapas $2–$15. AE, MC, V. Thurs–Fri 4:30–11pm, Sat 11am–11pm, Sun 11am–9pm.*

Where to **Dine**

★★ Alexandra GUANICA *INTERNATIONAL* The kitchen leans heavily on seafood and local flavors as it churns out tasty and inventive creations in an ambience of relaxed glamour. *Copamarina Beach Resort, Rte. 333 Km 6.5, Caña Gorda.* ☎ *787/621-0505. Entrees $18–$36. AE, DC, MC, V. Dinner daily.*

★ Blue Marlin GUANICA *SEAFOOD/PUERTO RICAN* Gorge on delicious seafood and have some drinks with the locals at this friendly restaurant in a converted plantation home on the town's main harbor, or malecón. *Calle Esperanza Idrach 55 (end of Calle 25 de Julio).* ☎ *787/821-5858. Entrees $9.50–$24. AE, MC, V. Lunch & dinner Thurs–Mon.*

★ kids La Casita LA PARGUERA *SEAFOOD* A simple family restaurant specializing in fresh seafood served in a half-dozen varieties, all of them delicious. *Calle Principal 304.* ☎ *787/899-1681. Entrees $8–$12. AE, MC, V. Lunch & dinner Tues–Sun.*

★★ La Cava PONCE *INTERNATIONAL* The restaurant mixes old-fashioned charm, evident in the

Mark's at the Melía.

service and decor, and gourmet European food to deliver one of this southern city's best dining experiences. *Ponce Hilton. Av. Caribe 1150.* ☎ *787/259-7676. Entrees $26–$35. AE, DC, DISC, MC, V. Dinner Mon–Sat.*

★ Galloway's BOQUERON *CREOLE/ CONTINENTAL* Time your meal to watch the sunset from the back-dock dining room overlooking the bay (6pm in the winter, 7pm in the summer), the perfect spot to enjoy wonderful seafood and surprisingly good continental entrees. Or dig into more relaxed pastas and pub fare at the front bar, which draws a convivial crowd. *Calle José de Diego.* ☎ *787/254-3302. Entrees $8–$26. AE, MC, V. Lunch & dinner daily; closed Wed.*

★★ Mark's at the Melía PONCE *INTERNATIONAL* Award-winning chef Mark French prepares haute cuisine with fresh Puerto Rican herbs and produce at this downtown landmark. *Hotel Melía. Calle Cristina.* ☎ *787/284-6275. Entrees $20–$40. AE, MC, V. Lunch & dinner Tues–Sat; brunch Sun.*

★ Tapas Café SAN GERMAN *SPANISH* A charming, sophisticated spot at the historic heart of this west-coast town, the restaurant serves large portions of tasty tapas and classics like paella. *Calle Dr. Santiago Vevé 50.* ☎ *787/264-0610. Tapas/ entrees $2–$20. AE, MC, V. Dinner Thurs–Sun; lunch Sat–Sun.*

Where to **Stay**

★ Bahia Salinas Beach Resort & Spa CABO ROJO This upscale, intimate inn is surrounded by a man-grove reserve, bird sanctuaries, and salt flats in the undeveloped coastal region near the Cabo Rojo Light-house. Salt mineral waters, similar

Copamarina Beach Resort.

to those of the Dead Sea, supply water for the onsite Jacuzzi and for treatments at its Cuni Spa, which gives a full range of beauty and relax-ation treatments. It also has excellent restaurants. Rooms have classic coun-try Puerto Rican furnishings. *Rd. 301 Km 11.5, Sector El Faro.* ☎ *787/254-1212. www.bahiasalinas.com. 22 units. Doubles $193–$205. AE, MC, V.*

★★ Copamarina Beach Resort GUANICA Surrounded by the Guánica Dry Forest and its undevel-oped coastline, this two-story, low-slung resort is perhaps the island's most quintessentially Caribbean property, right down to its red roof-ing and the verandas and terraces surrounding the property. It offers lots to do, from diving or bird-watch-ing to simply enjoying the large pool and lush grounds. It's popular with locals and European travelers looking for low-key comfort and good value. *Rte. 333 Km 6.5, Caña Gorda (P.O.*

Parador Guánica 1929.

Box 805). ☎ *888/881-6233 or 787/ 821-0505. www.copamarina.com. 106 units. Doubles $190–$285; villas $800–$1,000. AE, DC, MC, V. From Ponce, drive west along Rte. 2 to Rte. 116 & go south to Rte. 333, then head east.*

★ **kids Hilton Ponce Golf & Casino Resort** PONCE   The best full-service hotel on the south coast has a 28-hole golf course, sprawling pool area, lush grounds, and comfortable, spacious rooms with tasteful tropical style. There's a playground and pools for kids. The restaurants are among the city's best. *Av. Caribe 1150 (P.O. Box 7419).* ☎ *800/HILTONS or 787/259-7676. www.hilton.com. 153 units. Doubles $152–$419. AE, DC, DISC, MC, V.*

Meliá PONCE   Right on Ponce's central plaza, surrounded by its main historic sites, this basic hotel has small, comfortable rooms and a fine restaurant. Continental breakfast is served on a rooftop terrace. *Calle Cristina 2.* ☎ *800/448-8355 or 787/842-0260. www.hotelmeliapr. com. 73 units. Doubles $105–$115. Rates include breakfast. AE, MC, V.*

Parador Guánica 1929 GUANICA A classic Spanish-style plantation home, with a wide wraparound veranda on each of its two levels, its rooms have subdued tropical decor and are comfortable and well equipped. Breakfast is served on the downstairs side veranda overlooking the large pool area, with sun chairs on its surrounding deck. It lies on one of the island's prettiest roads, enveloped by a canopy of trees as it winds along Ensenada Bay and a line of plantation homes atop a hill overlooking it. *Rte. 3116 Km 2.5, Av. Los Veteranos, Ensenada.* ☎ *787/821-0099 or 787/842-0260. www.tropical innspr.com. 21 units. Doubles $102. Rates include breakfast. AE, MC, V.*

kids Parador Villa Parguera LAJAS   For years, this has been La Parguera's best property, with comfortable rooms, a pool, a boat dock, and a full-service restaurant that has live shows on weekend evenings. *Main St. 304 (P.O. Box 3400), Carretera 304 Km 303, La Parguera.* ☎ *787/ 899-7777. www.villaparguera.net. 74 units. Doubles $107–$165. AE, DC, DISC, MC, V. Drive west along Rte. 2 until you reach the junction with Rte. 116; then head south along Rte. 116 & Rte. 304.*

Mayagüez

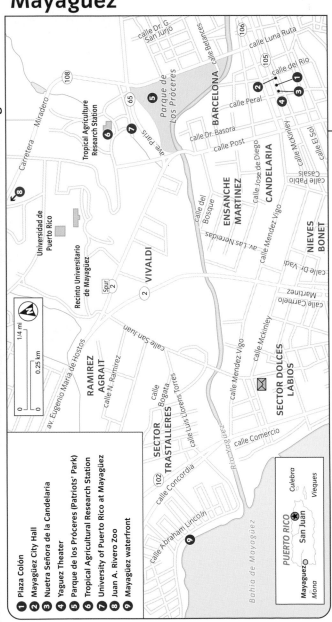

1 Plaza Colón
2 Mayagüez City Hall
3 Nuetra Señora de la Candelaria
4 Yaguez Theater
5 Parque de los Próceres (Patriots' Park)
6 Tropical Agricultural Research Station
7 University of Puerto Rico at Mayagüez
8 Juan A. Rivero Zoo
9 Mayagüez waterfront

Mayagüez lies in the middle of Puerto Rico's west coast, a major zone for fun in the sun, but lacks its own quality beach. It makes a convenient base to explore the region, however, equally close to the rougher Atlantic beaches to the north (Rincón, Aguadilla, and Isabela) and the calmer, clear waters of the Caribbean to the south (Cabo Rojo, Lajas, and Guánica).

It also has a number of sites that are worth a stop right in the city, which forged its own architectural style through successive renovations following a string of disasters, including a great fire in 1841 and a 1918 tsunami. START: **Plaza Colón, downtown Mayagüez.**

❶ The city's elegant central **Plaza Colón** is surrounded by restored historic buildings and is dominated by the bronze Columbus monument at its center, wide mosaic-tiled walkways and gurgling fountains, blooming tropical gardens, and squat leafy trees.

❷ and ❸ The plaza is home to the noteworthy neo-Corinthian **Mayagüez City Hall** and **Nuestra Señora de la Candelaria,** the latter of which has gone through several incarnations since the first building went up in 1780.

From Plaza Colón, walk west along Calle McKinley, its southern border, until you get to the corner of Calle Dr. Basora. Turn left, and a half a block down on the corner of Calle La Candelaria is:

❹ The recently restored **Yaguez Theater,** a neoclassical jewel that served as both an opera and silent movie house and is still in active use today. Originally inaugurated in 1909, a fire destroyed the structure in 1919; but it was rebuilt. The city's smashing **Art Deco post office** is also located here.

Head north along Calle Dr. Basora 6 full blocks and turn right at Calle Morell Campos.

❺ **Parque de los Próceres (Patriots' Park)** is on the banks of the Río Yaguez, the river that gives the city its name. Beautiful gardens, forested walkways, and a long row of commemorative plaques of Puerto Rico's historic figures mark the experience. *Located btw rtes. 65 & 108.*

Return to Calle Dr. Basora and continue north along Calle Post, which will pass over the river and onto Rte. 65. Turn right.

❻ The **Tropical Agricultural Research Station** is not a botanical garden but a working research facility of the U.S. Department of Agriculture. Get a free map at the administration office and explore the huge tropical plant species collections. The grounds contain cacao, fruit trees, spices, timbers, ornamentals, a palm plantation, and

Plaza Colón.

Juan A. Rivero Zoo.

a bamboo forest. *2200 Av. Pedro Albizu Campos (on Rte. 65 btw Post St. & Rte. 108).* ☎ *787/831-3435. Free admission. Mon–Fri 9am–5pm.*

Head west along Rte. 65 and onto Hwy. 2 for a few kilometers to reach:

❼ The **University of Puerto Rico at Mayagüez** (along Rte. 65, btw Post St. and Rte. 108), which is a charming, tree-covered campus known for its engineering and science curricula.

Return east along Hwy. 2 and Rte. 65, turning left at Rte. 108. Take a right at Calle Bonet to:

❽ **Juan A. Rivero Zoo.** This is a full zoo with an African safari exhibit that has lions, elephants, zebras, and rhinos. Jaguars are part of a Caribbean exhibit. There's also a butterfly and lizard exhibit and gorgeous grounds spread across 14 acres (5.6 hectares). The birdhouse

has a fantastic elevated walkway where you look down on colorful tropical birds such as parrots. There are also eagles, hawks, and owls. You can see the entire zoo in 2 hours. *Rte. 108, Barrio Miradero, Mayagüez Union.* ☎ *787/834-8110. Adults $6, 11–17 $4, 5–10 $2, 4 & under free. Wed–Sun & holidays 8:30am–5pm.*

It's a weaving but worthwhile journey from the downtown area to the city's waterfront.

Head east along Calle McKinley and go left on Calle Río South. Take a left onto Calle Mendez Vigo and then right at Av. González Clemente. Turn left at Calle San Pablo, which bears right and turns into Blvd. del Carmen. Turn right at Calle Rafael Nazario.

❾ The jewel of Mayagüez's **historic waterfront** district, with its rows of neat warehouses, is the restored 1920s **Custom House** located here.

Mayagüez beach.

Where to **Stay & Dine**

El Castillo *INTERNATIONAL/ PUERTO RICAN* This place adds flavor and flair to its classic seafood stews, surf and turf, and seafood delights like grilled salmon with a mango-flavored Grand Marnier sauce. *In the Mayagüez Resort & Casino. Rte. 104 Km 0.3.* ☎ *787/832-3030. Breakfast buffet $13; Mon–Fri lunch buffet $16; Sun brunch buffet $27; main courses $14–$36. AE, MC, V. Daily 6:30am–midnight.*

Howard Johnson Downtown Mayagüez This converted monastery is a charming historic hotel right near Plaza Colón. With its wide tiled walkways wrapped around an interior courtyard and Spanish colonial furnishings, this hotel is at home in the city's prettiest neighborhood. The construction allows the breeze in and affords nice vistas of historic Mayagüez. A pool fills one courtyard, and the hotel is outfitted with high-speed Internet and other modern amenities. There's no restaurant on premises but there are several nearby, including the delectable **Ricomini Café** across the street, where guests have their free continental breakfast. It can get noisy on weekends. *Calle Mendez Vigo Este 57, Mayagüez.* ☎ *787/832-9191. Fax 787/832-9122. www.HoJo.com. 35 units. Year-round $85–$125 double, $140 suite. Rates include continental breakfast at neighboring bakery. AE, MC, V.*

★ **Mayagüez Resort & Casino** The city's best resort is sprawled across 20 acres (8 hectares) of hilly

Howard Johnson Downtown Mayagüez.

tropical grounds, with a river pool whimsically set among palms and boulders. The guest rooms have private balconies with great views. The hotel is the major entertainment center of Mayagüez. Its casino has free admission and is open 24 hours a day. *Rte. 104 Km 0.3 (P.O. Box 3781), Mayagüez.* ☎ *888/689-3030 or 787/832-3030. Fax 787/265-3020. www.mayaguez resort.com. 140 units. Year-round $189–$259 double, $335 suite. AE, DC, DISC, MC, V.*

Veranda Terrace *INTERNATIONAL* For a casual dining experience, try this airy terrace overlooking the tropical gardens of this hotel. It's a great spot for light fare and some drinks. Open daily 11am to 1am. *In the Mayagüez Resort & Casino, Rte. 104.* ☎ *787/831-7575.*

The Northwest

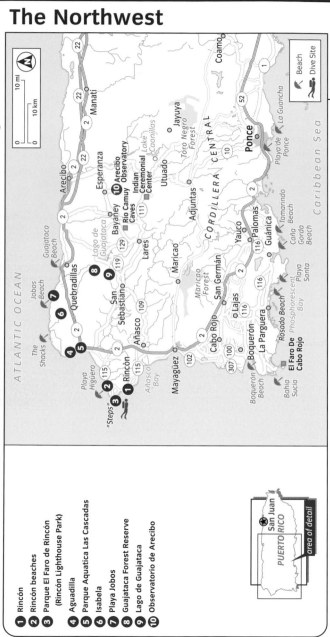

1 Rincón
2 Rincón beaches
3 Parque El Faro de Rincón
  (Rincón Lighthouse Park)
4 Aguadilla
5 Parque Aquatica Las Cascadas
6 Isabela
7 Playa Jobos
8 Guajataca Forest Reserve
9 Lago de Guajataca
10 Observatorio de Arecibo

Beach
Dive Site

PUERTO RICO
San Juan
area of detail

Puerto Rico's northwest coast is a land of vertiginous cliffs and powerful surf that pounds against beautiful beaches. Gorgeous natural attractions like lakes and caverns offer a variety of activities for visitors; and lively beachfront resorts, sleepy guesthouses, and coastal nightlife keep them entertained. START: **Head north of Mayagüez along Hwy. 2. At Rte. 115, exit toward Rincón.**

1 The resort town of **Rincón** is the first of a string of beach destinations you'll encounter as you head north. It lies at the western end of a piece of land jutting off the island's west coast, with La Cadena Hills running through its center and beautiful beaches surrounding it on three sides. It's still a sleepy coastal village attracting surfers and bohemian travelers, but it has become decidedly upscale in the last decade with new luxury vacation resorts.

To explore the town's beaches, take Rte. 413 as you get into town, which circles the town's coast, passing by nearly every major beach.

2 Rincón has **8 miles (12.8km) of beachfront,** with dozens of quirkily named beaches: Maria's, Indicator, Domes, The Point, Steps-Tres Palmas, Dog Man's. Part of the town's appeal is that it has both rough surfing beaches as well as tranquil Caribbean coastal areas,

better suited for swimming and snorkeling. Many beaches even provide both, depending on the time of year, or just the day. See chapter 6.

3 Adjacent to Domes is the **Parque El Faro de Rincón (Rincón Lighthouse Park),** the perfect spot to see endangered humpback whales winter here from December to March. A row of coin-operated binoculars lines a promenade along the town's western coast, looking out over the Mona Passage. The park is closed from midnight to 7am. There's a snack bar and souvenir shop. *Barrio Puntas, Carretera 413 Km 3.3.*

Take Rte. 115 out of town to the north until you hook up with Rte. 111, which takes you into Aguadilla.

4 **Aguadilla** is the biggest town on Puerto Rico's northwest corner, which is filled with great beaches and other natural blessings for an active

Swimmers at Crash Boat Beach.

vacation experience. And it makes a good base from which to explore the area, with lots of hotels, restaurants, good infrastructure, a fairly large mall, and lots of attractions, like a water park and golf course. The region also is near major attractions like the **Arecibo Observatory** and the **Río Camuy Cave Park.** In addition to its coast, there are mountain forests and lakes nearby. See p 105 and 145, respectively.

Take Hwy. 2 north out of Agua-dilla a few kilometers to get to:

⑤ The Parque Aquatica Las Cascadas (Hwy. 2 Km 126.5, Agua-dilla; ☎ 787/819-0950 or 787/819-1030). Kids will love this municipally run water park. It brims with giant slides, tubes, and the Río Loco rapids pool. The drawback is that it is open only from May through September (10am–5pm daily, 10am–6pm week-ends). Tickets are $16 for adults and $14 for kids (ages 4–12) plus a $5 tube-rental fee.

Proceed north along Hwy. 2 until you intersect with Rte. 112, which you will take to Isabela.

⑥ Isabela also has a beautiful coastline, riddled with wide beaches and great surf spots.

Sinkholes dot the rocky coast.

Isabela surfing.

From the downtown area, take the coastal Rte. 466 to visit the best beach spots.

⑦ Playa Jobos is the soul of this north-coast surf town, cherished more by the locals than by the expa-triates who have made Rincón their own. There's a wide sandy beach and beautiful sinkholes among the limestone hills surrounding it.

From Jobos, take Rte. 446 south, following it across Hwy. 2. It will eventually lead to:

⑧ Guajataca Forest Reserve in the mountains south of town, about 40 minutes from the coast.

The Department of Natural and Envi-ronmental Resources has an office along this roadway that has good maps with hiking routes through the reserve, about 2,400 acres (960 hect-ares) of forest that is home to nearly 50 species of birds, sprawling across mountains, rising and falling at vari-ous elevations, ranging from 500 to 1,000 feet (150–300m) or more.

Guajataca Forest Reserve is punctu-ated by *mogotes,* or limestone hills, and covered with 25 miles (40km) of hiking trails. It is also home to the endangered Puerto Rico boa (you are unlikely to encounter one) and the habitat of nearly 50 different

Just for Leather Lovers

Lalin Leather Shop is the Caribbean's largest equestrian emporium. It sells beautiful saddles and bridles from the island and South America at great prices. They have plenty of cowboy and cowgirl duds, too. Customers from around the world find it worth it to buy it here and ship it home. *Av. Piñero 1617, Puerto Nuevo.* ☎ *787/781-5305. AE, MC, V.*

species of birds. A highlight is the **Cueva del Viento (Cave of the Wind),** which you can crawl into if you dare. Hiking trails are well marked by park rangers. *Bosque Estatal de Guajataca (Guajataca Forest), Dept. de Recursos Naturales Oficina.* ☎ *787/872-1045 or 787/999-2000. Rte. 446 Km 9, Barrio Llanadas. Daily 6am–6pm.*

Continue east along Rte. 446 and then turn left toward Rte. 476, which you will enter by bearing right. At Rte. 119, take a left; then turn right at Rte. 453. At the intersection of Calle Julio Nieves, turn right; then take a left on Calle Lola Vera; and then a right at Calle P. Nieves. After bearing left, it becomes Calle Juan Vera, which winds right then left before coming to the beautiful lake.

9 The **Lago de Guajataca** is Puerto Rico's most beautiful lake. In a majestic setting, surrounded by green mountains, it is the perfect spot for relaxation. In fact, it's my favorite lake for some R&R on the island. It is both a 4-mile-long (6.4km) body of water and a wildlife refuge. For a scenic look at the lake, drive along its north shore, which is a haven for island freshwater anglers. You can go fishing here, but you have to bring your own equipment. The most sought-after fish is tucunare, with which the lake is stocked. At the dam here, you can gaze upon

an evocative "lost valley" of conical peaks.

Return to Hwy. 2 and take it heading east toward Arecibo. Continue until you pick up De Diego Expressway (PR 22) heading east. Take Rte. 129 south toward Utuado. Go left on Calle 1 and take a right on Rte. 651. At Rte. 635, take a left, and then go left on Rte. 625, which you will follow to the entrance of the observatory.

10 ★ **Observatorio de Arecibo** is home to the world's largest and most sensitive radar/radio-telescope, which features a 20-acre (8-hectare) dish, or radio mirror, set in an ancient sinkhole. It's 1,000 feet (300m) in diameter and 167 feet (50m) deep, and it is used by scientists as part of the Search for Extraterrestrial

Fishing in a mountain lake.

Intelligence (SETI) project, featured in the movie *Contact* with Jodie Foster. The 10-year, $100-million search for life in space was launched on October 12, 1992, the 500-year anniversary of the New World's discovery by Columbus, and supposes that advanced civilizations elsewhere in the universe might also communicate via radio waves.

Lush vegetation flourishes under the giant dish, and you can inspect it from a platform suspended above. There's a good visitor center with interactive exhibitions on solar systems, meteors, and other weather phenomena, and a souvenir shop on the grounds. Plan to spend about 1½ hours at the observatory. *Rte. 625 Final, Arecibo.* ☎ *787/878-2612. www.naic.edu. Wed–Sun 9am–4pm.*

Arecibo Observatory.

In winter (Dec 15–Jan 15) & summer (June 1–July 31) daily 9am–4pm. $5 adults, $3 seniors & children.

Where to **Dine**

★ **Parador Vistamar** QUEBRADIL-LAS *PUERTO RICAN* Located inside a hotel perched on an oceanside cliff, this restaurant serves basic local fare at decent prices in a dining room with an epic view—a good place to stop for a meal while on the road. *Rte. 2 & Rte. 113.* ☎ *787/895-2065. Entrees $8–$25. AE, DISC, MC, V. Dinner daily.*

★★ **Smiling Joe's** RINCON *CARIB-BEAN FUSION* Inventive fusion cooking served in beautiful, laid-back surroundings. *Lazy Parrot Inn, Rd. 413 Km 4.1, Barrio Puntas.* ☎ *787/*823-0101. Entrees $19–$33. AE, DISC, MC, V. Dinner daily.

★ **Tamboo Tavern and Seaside Grill Restaurant** RINCON *AMERICAN-CARIBBEAN* Dine amidst sand dunes and palm trees while watching the young and beautiful beach crowd. You can find just about everything on the menu, but stick to fresh seafood liked grilled Caribbean lobster and mahimahi in caper sauce. *Carretera 413 Km 4, Sandy Beach.* ☎ *888/823-8550. Entrees $16–$26. AE, MC, V. Lunch & dinner Thurs–Tues.*

Where to **Stay**

★★★ **Horned Dorset Primavera** RINCON This sophisticated hotel, with Spanish hacienda style, is set in a dreamscape of coastline and lush gardens, which the accommodations suited for aristocrats try hard to compete with. For years, this has been one of the Caribbean's most luxurious properties. Units have private plunge pools or sun decks. *Apdo.*

1132. ☎ 800/633-1857 or 787/823-4030. www.horneddorset.com. 55 units. Doubles $260–$1,070. AE, MC, V. Children under 12 not accepted.

The Lazy Parrot RINCON This is one of Rincón's best spots to stay, but pay the extra cash for one of the upstairs "panoramic" rooms for a view of the Cadena Hills and the coast—and more privacy. The pool makes up for the inland location, and the two restaurants are top rate. It's a good spot to find out what's going on around town from locals and expats. *Rd. 413 Km 4.1, Barrio Puntas.* ☎ 800/294-1752 or 787/823-5654. www.lazyparrot.com. 21 units. Doubles $99–$165. Rates include breakfast. AE, DISC, MC, V.

Lemontree Waterfront Suites RINCON You can hear the sound of the surf just outside your private back porch at these furnished and colorful seaside suites in various sizes with kitchen facilities. *Rte. 4290 (P.O. Box 3200).* ☎ 888/418-8733 or 787/823-6452. Fax 787/823-5821. www.lemontreepr.com. 6 units. Doubles $165–$195, 2-bedroom apt $265, 3-bedroom apt $295. AE, MC, V.

kids Marriott Courtyard Aguadilla AGUADILLA The pool and aquatics playground and the big rooms are attractive for families, but it's a great place for everyone, right near top beaches and attractions like the Camuy Caves. Nearby in Aguadilla there's a water park, a golf course, and an ice-skating rink. *West Parade/Belt Rd., Antigua Base Ramey.* ☎ 800/321-2211 or 787/658-8000. www.marriott.com. 152 units. Doubles $169–$199. AE, MC, V.

Rincón Beach Resort ANASCO A beautiful property with an infinity pool, fine beach, and large rooms and furnished apartments. It's a bit far removed from the rest of Rincón, but there's not much cause to leave, with a fine restaurant and lots of watersports activities. *Rte. 115 Km 5.8.* ☎ 866/598-0009 or 787/589-9000. www.rinconbeach.com. 118 units. Doubles $205–$280, 1-bedroom suite $459–$570, 2-bedroom suite $570–$650. Rates include continental breakfast. AE, DISC, MC, V.

★ Villa Montana Beach Resort ISABELA Caribbean-style plantation villas—with cathedral ceilings, peaked tin roofs, courtyards, and verandas—spread along a 35-acre (14 hectare) beachfront plot with two pools, a 3-mile (4.8km) beach, and surrounding tropical forests. There's something for everyone here: horseback riding, biking, health club, spa, and every watersport you can imagine. You can also hike through tropical forests or use the climbing wall on the property. There are also sports facilities such as basketball courts. *Carretera 4466 Km 1.9, Barrio Bajuras.* ☎ 888/780-9195 or 787/872-9554. www.villamontana.com. 60 units. Doubles $200–$400. AE, MC, V.

Horned Dorset Primavera.

The Central Mountains

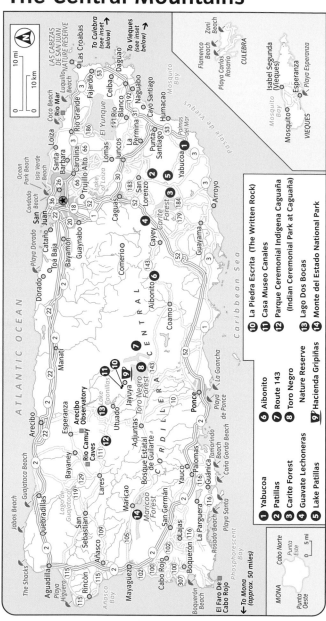

1. Yabucoa
2. Patillas
3. Carite Forest
4. Guavate Lechoneras
5. Lake Patillas
6. Aibonito
7. Route 143
8. Toro Negro
   Nature Reserve
9. Hacienda Gripiñas
10. La Piedra Escrita (The Written Rock)
11. Casa Museo Canales
12. Parque Ceremonial Indígena Caguaña
    (Indian Ceremonial Park at Caguaña)
13. Lago Dos Bocas
14. Monte del Estado National Park

The Panoramic Route is a tangle of narrow country roads crisscrossing Puerto Rico's mountainous interior from the east to west coasts. This route stretches for 165 miles (266km) over more than 40 country roads zigzagging in wide circles throughout the central mountains and can be driven at a leisurely pace over 3 days, from its beginnings outside the east-coast town of Yabucoa to its end in the damp cool of coffee country, between Maricao and Mayagüez.

Alternate routes through the mountains are also enjoyable, however, and it's also possible to pick up portions of the Panoramic Route outside major highways, like Hwy. 52 or Hwy. 10. **START: Yabucoa.**

1 Yabucoa is the eastern starting point of the Panoramic Route. It rises from the coast along sun-scorched cliffs with a magnificent view of the Caribbean.

From Rte. 3 south, take Rte. 182 toward Patillas to begin your ascent along this scenic mountain network.

2 You will climb through the coast to the green hills of **Patillas,** with the roadway cutting through beautiful forest as it climbs into the island's heart.

From Rte. 182, you will need to crisscross along Rte. 181 north, then Rte. 7740 west, and then Rte. 184.

3 The 6,000-acre (2,400-hectare) **Carite Forest** is a nature reserve with picnic and camping areas and a famous pond to take a dip in called Charco Azul (Blue Pond). Many gurgling mountain streams and small rivers run through the forest surrounding it.

4 Outside the forest reserve is a string of **lechoneras,** with live country music and salsa on weekends, which draw *sanjuaneros* hungry for some fresh mountain air and roast pork.

Continue along Rte. 184, turning left on Rte. 174. This road becomes Rte. 742.

Yabucoa.

5 You will come to **Lake Patillas,** one of the largest and prettiest lakes in the south. You can fish for bass in this reservoir, which is stocked by the commonwealth government.

Continue west on Rte. 742, turning left at Rte. 741, which you will take until Rte. 7741, where you will take a right and then continue until Rte. 15, which will take you into Cayey. Continue on, taking Rte. 14 toward Aibonito.

6 Aibonito, the highest town in Puerto Rico at 2,500 feet (750m), is a beautiful town surrounded by mountains and known for its annual flower festival in June.

Lechonera.

Take Rte. 162 out of town, which you can pick up from Rte. 14. It will wind upward toward Rte. 143.

7 **Route 143** is the heart of the Panoramic Route. This 30-mile (48km) stretch traverses the spine of the Cordillera Central mountain range, with views clear down to the northern and southern coasts on either side of the roadway.

8 The scenic route then follows its crooked but breathtaking course until it brings you to a treasure buried deep in the island's center: the 7,000-acre (2,800 hectare) **Toro**

Winding road in the Cordillera Central mountains.

Negro Nature Reserve, which sprawls across lush mountain forest that is every bit as impressive as El Yunque, with rivers, lakes, and crashing waterfalls cutting through the green jungle. Spend the rest of the afternoon exploring the reserve. The Doña Juana recreational area at the main entrance to the forest has a swimming pool filled with cold water from the mountain streams, a picnic area, and a rustic campground. An adjacent restaurant serves up Puerto Rican barbecued chicken and pork along with other local delicacies.

Make the 2-mile (3.2km) hike to the 200-foot (60m) **Doña Juana Falls,** which is well worth the effort. Many other hiking trails originate from this area.

Toro Negro spans over a variety of forest types and includes a towering palm forest and a misty mountain cloud forest.

The reserve is home to both the island's highest lake, the beautiful **Lago Guineo,** and the highest mountain, the 4,390-foot (1,317m) **Cerro de Punta.** It's an enjoyable half-hour ascent—and it rewards you with the best view in Puerto Rico, especially on a clear day.

Return east along Rte. 143 to Rte. 149, and take that north, farther into the central mountains to Rte. 144, which you'll take back west to access Jayuya. The area is filled with old coffee estates and lush mountain forest. Spend the night at:

9 Hacienda Gripiñas. Set amidst 20 acres (8 hectares) of coffee fields and nature, this charming respite in the cool mountain countryside is a great place to unwind or seek some relief from the heat.

The next morning, go west along Rte. 144. Before leaving town, you will want to see:

10 La Piedra Escrita (the Written Rock), a huge boulder beside a stream, with Taíno petroglyphs carved into the stone. The **Cemi Museum** (Rte. 144 Km 9.3; ☎ 787/828-1241) has a collection of Taíno pottery and cemís, amulets sacred to the island's indigenous peoples.

11 The adjacent **Casa Museo Canales** (Rte. 144 Km 9.4; ☎ 787/828-1241) is a restored 19th-century coffee plantation home with

interesting exhibits. Both museums charge $1 adults, 50¢ for children, and are open from 9am–3pm daily. The town hosts an annual Indigenous Festival in November.

Continue along Rte. 144 outside Jayuya, taking it to Rte. 111 and into Utuado.

12 Here, you'll find the **Parque Ceremonial Indígena Caguaña (Indian Ceremonial Park at Caguaña),** a 1,000-year-old Taíno Indian place of recreation and worship. There are ancient *bateyes* (ball courts) and stone monoliths covered with petroglyphs. *Rte 111 Km 12.3.* ☎ *787/894-7300. Free admission. Daily 8am–4pm.*

Take Rte. 111 to Hwy.10 north. Then take a right onto Rte. 123 to head to the Utuado lake region.

13 The mountain town is also home to several lakes, including the U-shaped **Lago Dos Bocas,** a nice spot to fish, or to take a ride around the lake in one of the ferryboats plying the lake, which makes stops at the rustic restaurants scattered throughout its shore.

You will take another tangle of roads to get to Maricao. The

Toro Negro Nature Reserve.

Indian Ceremonial Rock at Caguaña.

35-mile (56km) trip will take an hour and a half along country roads. Take Rte. 129 to Rte. 111, continuing west along Rte. 128 and then Rte. 431. You will then take Rte. 4311 and Rte. 124 into town. Then head north along Rte. 120.

⓮ Monte del Estado National Park (Rte. 120 Km 13.2; ☎ 787/873-5632) is a picnic area and campground in the Maricao Forest, with pools fed by mountain streams, a 2,600-foot-tall (780m) stone observation tower, and more than 50 species of birds. The reserve has 18 rivers and streams cutting through it.

Maricao is filled with historic coffee plantations and remains a center of Puerto Rico's gourmet coffee country to this day.

Where to **Stay & Dine**

Casa Grande Mountain Retreat UTUADO This parador sprawls across a former 100-acre (40 hectare) coffee plantation in the lush tropical forest in the north-central mountains, surrounded by lakes and karst. The rooms in wooden cottages have stripped-down comfort and style, each with a balcony, hammock, and view. Because the spot is all about decompressing, there's no TV, telephone, or air-conditioning. Instead, there is yoga, meditation, and a freshwater pool. Really, the thing to do here is nothing. They have a fine on-site restaurant. *Rte. 612 Km 0.3.* ☎ *888/343-2272 or 787/894-3900. www.hotel casagrande.com. 20 units. Doubles $80–$90. AE, DISC, MC, V.*

Hacienda Gripiñas Set amidst 20 acres (8 hectares) of coffee fields

and nature, this charming respite in the cool mountain countryside is a great place to unwind or seek some relief from the heat. Laden with hammocks and rocking chairs, reading rooms and balconies, it also has a pool and several hiking trails. The restaurant serves good local food. *Rte. 527 Km 2.5, Jayuya.* ☎ *787/828-1717. www.haciendagripinas.com. 48 units. Year-round $75 weekdays, $90 weekends double. AE, MC, V.*

The Jájome Terrace CAYEY Another good restaurant in Cayey that offers solid food and fine views. It caters to day-trippers from the city. *Rte. 15 Km 18.6, Cayey.* ☎ *787/738-4016. AE, MC, V. Thurs–Sun noon–midnight.*

★ Parador Hacienda Juanita MARICAO This former coffee plantation is surrounded by mountains

Coffee Plantation.

and lush cloud forest. Take it all in from the restaurant's back veranda. The parador dates from 1836 and is a beautiful country inn with a good restaurant, pool, and comfortable rooms with ceiling fans. The ability to take long walks around the property and the nighttime cool are eternal draws. *Rte. 105 Km 23.5 (HC01 Box 8200).* ☎ *787/838-2550. Fax 787/838-2551. www.hacienda juanita.com. 21 units. $125 double. Rates include breakfast & dinner. Children 11 & under stay free in parent's room. AE, MC, V.*

★★ Parador Hacienda Juanita Restaurant MARICAO *PUERTO*

RICAN Get a table out back on the veranda overlooking the verdant grounds, the best spot at this restored coffee plantation that serves filling island food. *Rte. 105 Km 23.5.* ☎ *787/838-2551. Entrees $8–$26. AE, MC, V. Dinner daily.*

The Sand and the Sea Inn

CAYEY *INTERNATIONAL* This inn has been serving great meals in the countryside for decades. From seafood to steak, from French to Puerto Rican, the food is always good and the view even better. *Rte. 715, Cayey.* ☎ *787/738-9086. Main courses $20–$30. AE, MC, V. Sat & Sun noon–midnight.*

Fajardo & the East

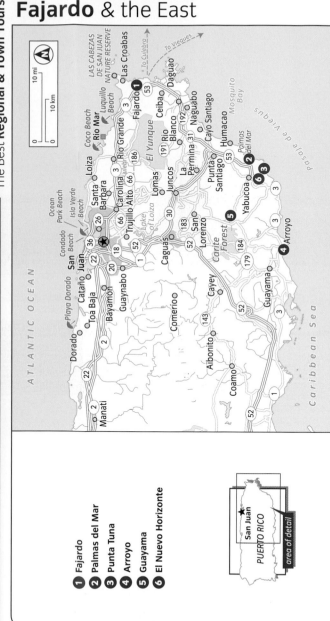

1 Fajardo
2 Palmas del Mar
3 Punta Tuna
4 Arroyo
5 Guayama
6 El Nuevo Horizonte

The eastern end of the island, only about 45 minutes from San Juan, contains the island's major attractions, El Yunque rainforest, two of the world's rare bioluminescent bays whose waters glow at night, and several great beaches, including Luquillo Beach and Seven Seas. There are also the island's top golf courses and resorts, so it makes a good spot to base yourself for a few days. START: Fajardo.

1 Fajardo, a preeminent sailor's haven, is actually part of a hub of islands, weaving through the neighboring Spanish Virgin Islands, and on to the U.S. and British Virgin Islands. The town has seven marinas as well as gorgeous beaches, snorkeling spots, and untamed forest.

Farther down the east coast is:

2 Palmas del Mar, an ever-growing resort and upscale vacation-home community on a wildly gorgeous beachfront.

Palmas del Mar.

The southeast, however, has small fishing towns, rural farmland, and quaint historic plazas surrounded by beautiful Spanish colonial architecture. The coast along this corner of Puerto Rico is still relatively undiscovered, despite the beauty of its unvarnished coastline and traditional towns. There are only a few small guesthouses. It can be easily visited in 1 day.

Punta Tuna lighthouse.

The area has deep sand beaches, powerful waves, and cliffs cutting across the landscape straight down to the coast. It's still possible to find empty beaches, but now there are more restaurants and lodging options than even a few years ago.

Take Hwy. 3 south from Humacao. In Yabucoa, pick up Rte. 901, a coastal road cutting along steep oceanfront cliffs and descending into Maunabo, a sleepy coastal village.

3 At **Punta Tuna,** along this road in town, there is a beautiful lighthouse built in 1892 and a wide public beach beside it with restaurants, restroom facilities, and an outdoor picnic area. It's among the best in the region. Elsewhere in town, the beaches are mostly deserted, used more by fishermen than beachgoers.

Beyond Maunabo, the main coastal road Rte. 3 travels through the pretty town of Patillas and then to:

4 **Arroyo,** the site of a public beach and government-run vacation center.

Rte. 3 continues on to:

5 **Guayama,** a once-important sugar town that has some beautiful Spanish colonial architecture. Time stands still at its downtown plaza, with beautifully restored buildings and a provincial air.

From here, Rte. 3 hooks up with Hwy. 52, the quickest way over the mountains and back into San Juan (a 45-min. drive).

6 **El Nuevo Horizonte** has great seafood and local cooking and the best view in southeast Puerto Rico—on a clear day you can see clear out to Vieques and the other islands. *See below.*

Where to **Dine**

★★ Chez Daniel HUMACAO *FRENCH* Faithfully allegiant classic French cuisine—bouillabaisse, onion soup, lobster, and chicken pies—is served at this restaurant along the Palmas del Mar Marina. *Marina Palmas del Mar.* ☎ *787/850-3838. Entrees $23–$42. AE, MC, V. Dinner Wed–Mon, lunch Fri–Sun.*

★★ El Nuevo Horizonte YABU-COA *PUERTO RICAN/SEAFOOD* Both dining room and deck have phenomenal views over the Caribbean. The house special is the *paella rey,* prepared to moist perfection and loaded with lobster, clams, shrimp, and mussels. The stuffed *mofongo* with seafood is among the island's best. *Rte. 901 Km 8.8.* ☎ *787/893-5492. Entrees $12–$45. AE, MC, V. Lunch & dinner Thurs–Sun.*

★★ Otello's FAJARDO *NORTHERN ITALIAN* Dine amidst marble and gold-leaf, nude Roman statues and frescos, all the while gorging on Italian classics, from veal to shellfish to pasta. *El Conquistador Resort.* ☎ *787/863-1000. Entrees $26–$43. AE, DC, DISC, MC, V. Dinner daily.*

★★ Palio RIO GRANDE *ITALIAN* A richly decorated restaurant that stays close to culinary tradition of the highest order. *Wyndham Río Mar Beach Resort & Golf Club, Río Grande.* ☎ *787/888-6000. Entrees $22–$52. AE, DC, MC, V. Dinner daily.*

★★ Soleil Beach Club PINONES *SEAFOOD/CONTINENTAL* Tables are scattered along terraces bathed in ocean breezes and within earshot of the waves. The seafood, local dishes, and Argentinean-style steaks are as good as the view. *Carretera 187 Km 4.6.* ☎ *787/253-1033. Entrees $18–$38. AE, DISC, MC, V. Lunch & dinner daily. Soleil Beach Club Van has free pickup & drop-off from hotels.*

★★ Stingray Café FAJARDO *CARIBBEAN FUSION* A deliciously crafted menu, heavy on seafood and continental classics with regional and Asian riffs, is available at this harborside restaurant on the Caribbean. *El Conquistador Resort.* ☎ *787/863-1000. Entrees $29–$50. AE, DISC, MC, V. Dinner daily.*

Where to **Stay**

★★★ 🔲 El Conquistador Resort & Golden Door Spa

FAJARDO   This tasteful, Mediterranean-inspired fantasy resort has its own funicular, water park, several pools in a breathtaking setting, a marina, a private ferry, and private island with caverns, nature trails, horseback riding, and watersports, plus beautiful beaches. The resort is divided into a main hotel, an upscale Andalusian village, and two resort communities, all tied together with lush landscaping. It also has full sports, spa, health, and beauty facilities. *Av. Conquistador 1000, Las Croabas.* ☎ *866/317-8932 or 787/863-1000. www.elconresort.com. 918 units. Doubles $179–$558. AE, DC, DISC, MC, V.*

El Yunque Rainforest Inn

This low-key virgin rainforest retreat is just 45 minutes from the airport, surrounded by El Yunque rainforest. The villa has an elegant lodge and is nicer than the chalet for couples. The management also offers a villa that sleeps four or more and has a pool. The inn serves breakfasts and has a library with books and movies, a Wi-Fi connection, and a house computer. You'll breathe in fresh air and really relax. *P.O. Box 2087, Río Grande. Call or e-mail for directions to the property.* ☎ *787/809-8426. www.rainforestinn.com. Chalet $135; villa $165; luxury villa $500. AE, DISC, MC, V.*

★ Four Points by Sheraton Palmas del Mar Resort

HUMACAO   This hotel is just what this famed vacation area needed. Rooms are spacious and handsome; so are the golf courses, country club, and infinity pool. *Candelero Dr. 170.* ☎ *787/850-6000. www.starwoodhotels.com. 107 units. Doubles $160–$240. AE, MC, V.*

★★★ 🔲 Gran Melia Puerto Rico

RIO GRANDE   This pocket of posh on the Miquillo de Río Grande peninsula fronts a pretty beach and is in the shadow of El Yunque Rainforest. Amenities—from golf to watersports—are tops. *Coco Beach Blvd. 1000.* ☎ *866/436-3542. www.gran-melia-puerto-rico.com. 582 units. Suites $264–$700. AE, DISC.*

★ Parador Palmas de Lucía

YABUCOA   This knockout discovery lies at the eastern end of Ruta Panorámica, a network of scenic, winding roads, and steps from the pretty Playa Lucía. *Palmas de Lucía, rtes. 901 & 9911, Camino Nuevo.* ☎ *787/893-4423. www.palmasdelucia.com. 34 units. Doubles $102. AE, MC, V. From Humacao, take Rte. 53 south to Yabucoa, to the end of the hwy., where you connect with Rte. 901 to Maunabo. After a 2-min. drive, turn left at the signposted Carretera 9911, which leads to Playa Lucía.*

Golfing at El Conquistador Resort.

The Best of **Vieques in Three Days**

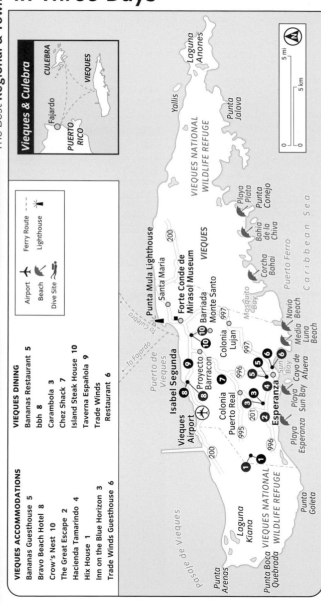

VIEQUES ACCOMMODATIONS

Bananas Guesthouse **5**
Bravo Beach Hotel **8**
Crow's Nest **10**
The Great Escape **2**
Hacienda Tamarindo **4**
Hix House **1**
Inn on the Blue Horizon **3**
Trade Winds Guesthouse **6**

VIEQUES DINING

Bananas Restaurant **5**
bbh **8**
Carambola **3**
Chez Shack **7**
Island Steak House **10**
Taverna Española **9**
Trade Winds
  Restaurant **6**

Airport ✈
Beach 🏖
Dive Site 🤿
Ferry Route - - -
Lighthouse 🗼

Vieques & Culebra

CULEBRA
VIEQUES
PUERTO RICO
Fajardo

0 — 5 mi
0 — 5 km

Vieques lies **7 miles (11km) off the northeast coast of Puerto Rico**. The 21-mile-long (34km) island has about 10,000 residents, charming villages and vacation homes, guesthouses and luxury lodgings, fabulous natural areas, and great beaches and offshore waters. The former military lands on its eastern and western ends now host nature reserves. START: **Isabel Segunda.**

1 Isabel Segunda. Named after Queen Isabella II, under whose reign the last Spanish fort in the Americas broke ground in 1843, this is the island municipality's main town, home to its ferry port, town hall, main square, and commercial downtown area.

Take care of your shopping and other needs here. A supermarket, drug and department stores, and a post office are in walking distance of the ferry port. Go right up the hill along the main road and bear left along Benitez Guzman, and then left on Calle Baldorioty de Castro. Turn right on Calle Muñoz Rivera to reach Morales Supermercado. This street is also home to hardware, department, and clothing stores, and the post office and main Banco Popular branch. Take Muñoz Rivera to Rte. 200, then take a left at Calle San Francisco and then another at Calle Fuerte.

2 Fort Conde de Mirasol Museum. The site of Spain's last military stand in the New World takes its name from the count who convinced the crown to build the fort in the 1840s. The carefully restored fortress is perched on a hill above Isabel Segunda. The town museum celebrates the history of Vieques—its Taíno past; the migration of French, Danish, and Spanish immigrants; and African slaves and former slaves. Find out about the great liberator Simón Bolívar and about the long struggle against the Navy presence. Museum curator Robert Rabin was a major figure in that movement.

Barriada Fuerte. at Magnolia 471. ☎ *787/741-1717. Wed–Sun 8:30am–4:20pm. Admission $2; free for ages 11 & under.*

3 Esperanza. Once a center for the island's sugarcane industry, Esperanza is now a pretty little fishing village, its streets lined with small guesthouses, restaurants, and bars, which provide the island's main nightlife.

To get there from Isabela Segunda, head right as you leave along Rte. 200, and then turn left at Rte. 201, which you take through the island's lush and hilly countryside. From the airport, take Rte. 200 east until it intersects with Rte. 201, and turn right onto it. After climbing through the interior's canopy-draped roadways, you will descend again to the island's south coast. Immediately afterward, turn left on Rte. 996 to get into town. At the

Fort Conde de Mirasol Museum.

Getting to & Around Vieques

Unless you're on a budget, skip the ferry and fly to Vieques, especially if your time is limited. The money you'll spend will buy you another day on one of its beautiful beaches—a worthy tradeoff for the cheap airfare. Flights to Vieques leave from Isla Grande Airport near the heart of San Juan as well as the main Luis Muñoz Marín International Airport near Isla Verde.

Vieques Air Link (☎ 888/901-9247 or 787/741-8331) has the most flights and the best prices. It operates three daily flights from LMM International as well as six flights from the smaller and more convenient Isla Grande Airport. The VAL flight from Isla Grande is about $98 round-trip, about half the rate from LMM International, which is $180. **Isla Nena** (☎ 787/741-8331) is an on-demand airline that flies to Vieques from LMM International (also $180 round-trip). **The Puerto Rico Port Authority** operates two ferries a day to Vieques from the eastern port of Fajardo; the trip takes about an hour. The round-trip fare is $4.50 for adults, $2 for children. Tickets for the morning ferry that leaves Saturday and Sunday sell out quickly, so you should be in line at the ticket window in Fajardo before 8am (it opens at 6:30am) to be certain of a seat on the 9am boat. Otherwise, you'll have to wait until the 1 or 3pm ferry. For more information about these sea links, call ☎ 800/981-2005, 787/863-0705 (Fajardo), or 787/741-4761 (Vieques). Ferries leave Fajardo for Vieques at 9:30am and 1, 4:30, and 8pm during the week and at 9am and 3 and 6pm on weekends and holidays.

Public cabs or vans called *públicos* transport people around the island. To fully experience Vieques, however, you should rent a jeep. The mountainous interior, more than a dozen beaches, and the nature reserves on former military bases absolutely require it. I recommend **Island Car Rental** (☎ 787/741-1666), **Marcos Car Rental** (☎ 787/741-1388), or **Martineau Car Rental,** Rte. 200 Km 3.2 (☎ 787/741-0078). Rates run about $50 per day. All the rental agencies will meet you at the airport or ferry if you prearrange a rental.

Vieques ferry.

Fishing boats in Esperanza.

intersection there is a small grocery and convenience store.

The main promenade runs along the harbor, and the main street along its side is lined with restaurants and guesthouses looking out on the charming harbor, with sailboats bobbing and cays lying just offshore. Local teens jump off the wooden pier, where modest wooden fishing boats and pleasure craft tie up.

④ ★ Sun Bay (Sombe) Public Beach. This government-run, panoramic crescent of sand—with picnic tables, a bathhouse, and an immense parking lot—is the most accessible of all of the island's beaches, but you can still find some solitude on weekdays along this spectacularly beautiful shore.

⑤ Drive through the large parking area that stretches across a huge swath of beach and follow the dirt road running along the beautiful shore. The road becomes increasingly rutted and winding as it snakes through coastal scrub forest to **Media Luna Beach** and **Navio Beach,** both protected coves that are fantastic swimming and snorkeling areas. A left fork leads to the muddy and rutted parking lot that

services Mosquito Bay (aka Phosphorescent Bay).

⑥ Mosquito Bay is one of the world's finest **phosphorescent bays.** At night, when the water is disturbed, these organisms dart, leaving trails of phosphorescence—called "whirling fire" since the time of the Taíno Indians. It's best to visit on moonless nights. A former Connecticut biology teacher runs **Island Adventures** (☎ 787/741-0720) aboard the nonpolluting *Luminosa.* You'll get a fine lesson on the bay's ecology but kayak trips are more fun. Most jaunts cost $30 and

Sun Bay Beach.

last about 2 hours. **Blue Caribe Kayak** (☎ 787/741-2522) is a good option.

Day 2 is all about beaches. To get to your first stop from Esperanza, head east out of town, taking the turnoff for Rte. 997 to the east. From Isabela Segunda, you'll take Rte. 200 to reach the main entrance to the wildlife reserve on the old Navy bombing range.

⑦ On May 1, 2003, the U.S. Navy transferred 15,500 acres (6,200 hectares)—including some of the island's best beachfront property—to the U.S. Fish & Wildlife Service, which added them to the **Vieques National Wildlife Refuge ★★★**. Wilderness areas now cover both the island's eastern end, home to marine training and bombing ranges, and its western end, a former Navy base and ammunition storage post. The western end has two fine beaches: Green Beach, in the northwest corner of the island beside a nature reserve, and a south-coast beach beside the ruins of the Playa Grande sugar plantation and the eerie Navy radar facility. Much of the land is run through with rows and rows of cement munition bunkers, and the military also left a huge pier, which originally was to form a bridge to the main island of Puerto Rico. (The attack on Pearl Harbor put a stop to the original plans.) The eastern end is more beautiful, with virgin coastline and brilliant blue ocean. Much of it, however, remains closed to visitors as the Navy cleans up the former training areas. Despite these scars, much of the landscape looks virgin, including the island's best white-sand beaches, upland forests, mangrove wetlands, and coral-reef and sea-grass beds that attract brilliant marine life. The refuge is open to the public and also contains a **Visitor Center at Vieques Office Park** (Rd. 200 Km 0.4; ☎ 787/741-2138). The refuge is open 7 days a week during daylight hours.

Biking through Vieques.

Kayaking in the wildlife refuge.

8 The best beaches are inside the Vieques National Wildlife Reserve, or the **Refugio Nacional de Vida Silvestre de Vieques** and include **Red Beach (Bahia Corcha), Blue Beach (Bahia de la Chiva),** and **Playa Plata.** Take the entrance off Rte. 997 and head straight for about a mile, bearing right to Red Beach (Bahia Corcha), which has shaded picnic tables and portable restroom facilities and is a good spot for families. **Blue Beach (La Chiva)** is more secluded, a series of small beaches and bathing spots hidden by mangrove and coastal forest. Other, similar spots

Vieques After Dark

Al's Mar Azul (On the waterfront, adjacent to the ferryboat piers, in Isabel Segunda; ☎ 787/741-3400) draws expatriates from the states who have settled here, but also is a hit with local *viequenses* and visitors. As such, it's a great spot for travel tips (check out the bulletin board packed with useful info). Overlooking the sound between the island and Puerto Rico's east coast, this waterfront pub is right next to the ferry, so it is practically an obligatory stop. Al actually exists; the burly owner often calls drink specials on the fly and has been known to occasionally don one of the bras hanging amidst the fishnets and nautical decor. For a different vibe, check out **Bar Plaza** (Plaza del Recreo, Isabel Segunda; ☎ 787/741-2176), a Spanish colonial tavern on the main plaza. With high ceilings and slowly whirring fans, the double doors are left slung open, which helps the clientele cool off with the icy-cold beers. La NASA (no phone, on the harbor at Esperanza) is nothing more than a wooden shack serving cold beers and rum and Cokes. But there's no place finer to have a drink than from the plastic chairs in the backroom overlooking the tranquil harbor. It's the place to go on weekend nights.

Vieques fishermen.

are spread along the coast to **Playa Plata,** the last beach along this coast open to the public, which has sea-grape and palmetto trees. Spend the day enjoying these beaches and discovering Vieques's coastal wildlife.

Spend your third day actively exploring Vieques, either above or below the waves. Your adventure will start at your hotel or favorite breakfast spot, where any of the operators below will pick you up at a specified time.

Vieques lighthouse.

⑨ Adventures at Sea. Blue Caribe Kayaks (Calle Flamboyan 149, Esperanza; ☎ 787/741-2522; www.bluecaribekayaks.com) offers kayaking, snorkeling, light tackle fishing, and night tours of the island's bioluminescent bay. Kayak rentals are $25 to $35 for a half-day; snorkeling gear is $12 daily. Kayak snorkeling tours lasting 2½ hours are $30 per person; half-day spin-casting fishing tours from kayaks are $60 per person.

Nan-Sea Charters (P.O. Box 1278, Vieques; ☎ 787/741-2390; www.nanseacharters.com) is an experienced scuba-trip operator and certified instructor that also offers sightseeing tours and charters on its 28-foot (8.4m) covered boat. Half-day, two tank dives cost $100 per person and a resort course is $125. They also offer half-day and full-day snorkeling tours.

⑩ Adventures on Land. Vieques Adventure Company (no physical address; ☎ 787/692-9162; www.bikevieques.com) leads mountain-bikers on half-day ($75 per person) and full-day ($105 per person) tours of the remote trails that barrel through the island's natural beauty. Depending on your crew, rides can include technically difficult and tiring treks for those who dare, but more subtle forays are also possible. The company also rents bikes and sea kayaks and runs fabulous saltwater fly-fishing tours at a price of $150 for a half-day.

Where to **Dine**

★★ **Carambola** INTERNATIONAL On the premises of the Inn on the Blue Horizon (see below), this restaurant serves the best food on Vieques. Also onsite is a bar that a team of journalists declared as one of their favorites in the world, so consider starting your evening with a drink or two in the octagonal Blue Moon Bar. Meals are served within the inn's main building or beneath an awning on a seafront terrace lined with plants. I love the pork loin in rum chutney and the daily stuffed *mofongo* special. Expect a crowd of fashion-industry folk, temporarily absent from New York and Los Angeles, and local residents mixing gregariously. *In the Inn on the Blue Horizon. Rte. 996 Km 4.3.* ☎ *787/741-3318. Reservations required. Main courses $24–$33. AE, MC, V. 1 mile (1.6km) west of Esperanza. Dinner Wed–Sun. Map p 118.*

Island Steak House FLORIDA INTERNATIONAL   Set in the cool and breezy highlands of Vieques on a verdant hillside with sweeping views of the island's interior, this restaurant is perched within a gracefully proportioned open-sided building that gives the impression of something midway between a simplified gazebo and a treehouse. Menu items include four different kinds of steak, lamb chops, chicken breasts stuffed with goat cheese and cherry tomatoes, jumbo fried shrimp, and Vieques lobster basted with a sauce made from spiced rum and butter. *In the Crow's Nest Hotel. Rte. 201 Km 1.6, Barrio Florida.* ☎ *787/741-0033. Burgers $8–$9; main courses $17–$39. AE, MC, V. Dinner daily. Map p 118.*

Bananas Restaurant ESPERANZA INTERNATIONAL   This unpretentious place has a great location

Esperanza.

overlooking Esperanza's main street and harbor. Bar food and cold drinks sums up the offerings here, but everything is quite nicely done. *Calle Flamboyan (El Malecón), in Esperanza.* ☎ *787/741-8700. Salads & sandwiches $5–$11; main courses $15–$17. MC, V. Lunch & dinner daily. Map p 118.*

★★★ **bbh** *CARIBBEAN/INTERNA-TIONAL* This is a surprisingly sophisticated tapas restaurant at the ever-surprising Bravo Beach Hotel. You can dine by candlelight beside the pool while overlooking the sea. *In the Bravo Beach Hotel, North Shore, Rd. 1.* ☎ *787/741-1128. Main courses $7–$18. AE, DC, MC, V. Wed–Sat lunch, dinner; Sun brunch. Map p 118.*

Chez Shack ESPERANZA *INTERNA-TIONAL* Chez Shack brings the cool back into counterculture; it's a funky, brightly painted, rustic, wooden spot with a small bar, no-frills dining room, and great flavor.

Hugh Duffy, who has been operating such places in the Caribbean since Mama Cass waitressed at his Love Shack in St. Thomas, is often on hand spinning a tale. The food is always good, but save your night out here for Monday barbecue nights, with great food and a live band playing reggae music. *Rte. 995 north of Esperanza.* ☎ *787/741-2175. Main courses $18–$22. MC, V. Wed–Mon dinner. Map p 118.*

Taverna Española ISABEL SEGUNDA *SPANISH/PUERTO RICAN* Visitors find genuine island hospitality at this weathered Spanish seafood restaurant with a lot of character that's a local favorite. From the fried fresh fish in Creole sauce and the Spanish seafood stew, the food is worth the inevitable wait. *Calle Carlos Libron.* ☎ *787/741-1175. Main courses $12–$15. AE, MC, V. Dec–May breakfast, lunch & dinner daily; June–Nov Fri–Sun dinner. Map p 118.*

Where to **Stay**

Inn on the Blue Horizon.

★★ **Bravo Beach Hotel** VIEQUES This boutique hotel has rooms with terraces so close to the beach that you can hear its rhythm and taste its salt. It is fashionably minimalist and full of extras (like high-quality bath products and a poolside honor bar), but the best thing about it is the great sleep you'll get so near the sea. *North Shore Rd. 1, Bravos de Boston.* ☎ *787/741-1128. www. bravobeachhotel.com. 12 units. Doubles $190–$275, villas $550. AE, DC, MC, V. Map p 118.*

Crow's Nest FLORIDA Set high on 5 acres (2 hectares) of forested hillside, about 1½ miles (2.4km) west/southwest of Isabel Segunda, this inn unwinds easily around its beautiful pool area surrounded by hills. The comfortable, attractive units all have cooking facilities and the grounds are lovely. *Rte. 201 Km 1.6, Barrio Florida, Box 1521.* ☎ *787/741-0033. www.crows nestvieques.com. 17 units. Doubles $109–$135. AE, MC, V. Map p 118.*

★ **Hacienda Tamarindo** PUERTO REAL   This inn is decorated in *hacienda* style around a huge tamarind tree, which dominates its attractive atrium. It's a 5-minute walk to the beach down a sand path and a 10-minute walk to town. Children are not welcome. A large pool overlooks the undeveloped coast. *Rte. 996 Km 4.5, Barrio Puerto Real (P.O. Box 1569).* ☎ *787/741-0420. www. haciendatamarindo.com. 16 units. Doubles $135–$230. Rates include breakfast. AE, MC, V. Map p 118.*

★ **Hix House** VIEQUES   The minimalist structures here blend into 12 acres (4.8 hectares) of forested hillside surrounding this award-winning inn by Toronto-based architect John Hix. The rooms have no windows or air-conditioning, but rather mosquito netting and low-watt lighting. The concrete and hardwood furniture blends into the sturdy rooms spread out in four separate buildings. Open-air showers also bring you closer to nature. Rooms have refrigerators stocked with essentials and ceiling fans. *Rte. 995 Km 1.5, Vieques.* ☎ *787/741-2302. www. hixislandhouse.com. 13 units. Doubles $195–$310. AE, MC, V. Map p 118.*

★★ **Inn on the Blue Horizon**
VIEQUES   One of the finest places to stay on Vieques, it's located on a wide, flat bluff overlooking the beautiful southern coastline. The Mediterranean-style main building has a huge main lobby, with an outrageously high ceiling, overlooking an infinity pool and blue horizon

Vieques bar.

beyond. Rooms spread from the main house to a group of cottages, where the units have private balconies and sea views. The area is beautifully landscaped with bougainvillea and mosaic tile. The circular bar has a great view, as does an additional cliff-side bar and dining area. The restaurant, **Carambola,** is one of the island's most respected. *Rte. 996 Km 4.3, Vieques (P.O. Box 1556).* ☎ *787/741-3318. www. innontheblue horizon.com. 10 units. Doubles $130–$375. AE, MC, V. Map p 118.*

Trade Winds Guesthouse
ESPERANZA   Popular with divers and visitors from the main island, this clean, comfortable guesthouse offers good rates and a restaurant that serves the best breakfast in town. The restaurant and front terrace overlook the peaceful harbor. Some rooms also have terraces, but only half have air-conditioning. *Calle Flamboyan 107, Barrio Esperanza (P.O. Box 1012).* ☎ *787/741-8666. www.enchanted-isle.com/tradewinds. 11 units. Doubles $60–$90. AE, MC, V. Map p 118.*

The Best of **Culebra**

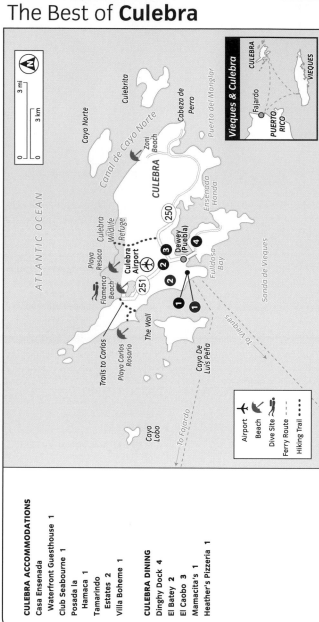

CULEBRA ACCOMMODATIONS

Casa Ensenada
Waterfront Guesthouse 1

Club Seabourne 1

Posada la
Hamaca 1

Tamarindo
Estates 2

Villa Boheme 1

CULEBRA DINING

Dinghy Dock 4

El Batey 2

El Caobo 3

Mamacita's 1

Heather's Pizzeria 1

This sun-bleached island is known for its stunning beaches and emerald waters, as well as its gorgeous countryside. Chic vacation homes and lodgings have appeared with its increasing popularity, but the island remains relatively rural and pastoral. At 7 miles (11km) long and 3 miles (5km) wide, the island has only 2,000 residents, and large swaths of it are wilderness areas protected from development. Note that although it is possible to see most of Culebra in a day, I recommend spending at least two days to see the island at a relaxed pace. START: **Dewey.**

1 The main town, **Dewey,** was named for Admiral George Dewey, a U.S. participant in the Spanish-American War, but locals call it *el pueblo*. Today, it is home to the ferry dock, where boats ply the route to the main island, as well as a clutch of guesthouses, restaurants, and small shops.

From the ferry dock, head down the main road (Rte. 250/Rte. 251) to Escudero, where you will turn right. Take your next left on an unmarked road to get to one of the Caribbean's nicest beaches.

2 The most popular beach is **Flamenco Beach,** a mile of the whitest sand you will ever see fronting

sapphire-colored sea. Although rustic by most standards, this is the most populous and developed beach on the island. There's a government-run campground where you can pitch a tent for $20 per night. There are also freshwater showers and bathrooms. For reservations, contact the **Flamenco Campground Office** (☎ 787/742-0700) or the **Culebra Conservation and Development Authority** (☎ 787/742-3880). A dirt road running along the beach has some freshwater tanks and vendors selling snacks and cold drinks.

Continue along the beachfront road and walk over a hill to get to:

Flamenco Beach.

Getting to & Around Culebra

Vieques Air Link (☎ 787/741-8331; www.viequesairlink.com) flies to Culebra twice a day from San Juan's Isla Grande Airport. The round-trip fare is $105. I recommend flying as you will spend the day traveling to get to the island otherwise.

The **Puerto Rico Port Authority** operates daily ferries from the mainland port of Fajardo to Culebra; the trip takes about an hour. The round-trip fare is $4.50 for adults, $2.25 for children 3 to 12 (2 and under free). For reservations, call ☎ 800/981-2005 or 787/863-0705 (in Fajardo).

With no public transportation, the only way to get to Culebra's beaches is by bike or a rental car. There are a number of companies; prearrange to be met at the airport. Rates range from $45 to $85 daily. Options include the following: **Carlos Jeep Rental** (Parcela 2, Barriada Clark, Dewey; ☎ 787/742-3514), **Coral Reef,** Carretera Pedro Marquez 3, Dewey; ☎ 787/742-0055), and **Willie's Jeep Rental** (Calle Escudero, Barriada Clark, Dewey; ☎ 787/742-3537).

❸ Playa Carlos Rosario. This is not as picturesque as Flamenco but is a renowned snorkeling spot. A quarter-mile south is **The Wall,** an offshore area with steep drop-offs that attract multitudes of fish.

❹ A drive along the island's few roadways leads past pretty coastal panoramas and fields of scrub forest and cacti, tropical plants, and towering palms. Travel

Abandoned tank on Flamenco Beach.

the entire, winding lengths of Rte. 250/Rte. 251 to see some of the island's beautiful coastal areas and get a sense of what the island has to offer. You can do the entire route at a leisurely pace in an hour.

❺ The **Culebra Wildlife Refuge** encompasses several plots on the main island and some 23 other off-shore islands. Much of the area is on former Navy training grounds. It's home to several bird colonies, including large seabirds like pelicans and boobies, as well as important turtle-nesting sites. **Culebrita,** a mile-long (1.6km) cay just off the coast, is a great snorkeling spot. It has a light-house and inviting beaches.

Take Rte. 250/251 all the way east, turning right on an unnamed road along the Puerto del Manglar Bay.

❻ The isolated **Zoni Beach** is located here, as popular with lovers as it is with snorkelers. During the week, it's often possible to have this picture-perfect stretch of white sand and aqua-blue ocean all to yourself.

Snorkeling.

7 Known for uncrowded, beautiful underwater vistas, Culebra has more than 50 choice dive sites, so ask a local where to go. **Culebra Divers** (Calle Escobar 138, Dewey; ☎ 787/742-0803; www.culebradivers.com) offers a two-tank dive for $95. It also offers a resort course for $95 or a 4-day PADI certification for $550 (equipment included with rates). **Jim Petersen's Ocean Safari** (Calle Escudero 189, Dewey; ☎ 787/379-1973) rents kayaks and will give you advice where to go, or he can take you on a tour to Culebrita or other spots, depending on conditions.

Where to **Dine**

Dinghy Dock DEWEY *PUERTO RICAN/CARIBBEAN* This spot is literally on the dock of the bay, near Dewey's drawbridge, a bar and restaurant that's open all day and serves everything from fruit waffles to fresh-caught grilled tuna. *Punta del Soldado Rd.* ☎ *787/742-0233. Main courses $5–$30. AE, MC, V. Breakfast, lunch & dinner daily. Map p 128.*

El Batey DEWEY *DELI* A bar serving deli sandwiches and bathed in the breeze and view from the bay. You can shoot pool and explore the jukebox. The spot really shakes on Friday and Saturday nights and goes old-school Puerto Rican dance hall on Sunday afternoons—that's bolero time. *Parque de Pelota 250, Carretera.* ☎ *787/742-3828. Sandwiches $3–$5. No credit cards. Wed–Sun lunch & dinner. Map p 128.*

Heather's Pizzeria DEWEY *PIZZA* This funky pizza place also serves salads, pastas, and sandwiches. Everything is good, and it's a hot spot for expats and visitors. The staff is friendly and full of good

advice. *Calle Marques 14, Dewey.* ☎ *787/742-3175. Pizzas, sandwiches & platters $9–$25. No credit cards. Wed–Sun dinner. Map p 128.*

Mamacita's DEWEY *ECLECTIC* A colorful spot right on the Dewey channel, this guesthouse/restaurant is known for its fine food, tropical decor, and lively back patio. Whether you're having coffee and French toast or a beer and grilled swordfish, this is a great spot to have it. The best rooms are the two suites with

Eating at Mamacita's.

kitchenettes, or the Crow's Nest on the top floor, opening onto a panoramic view. Rates are $95 double, or $105 to $135 suite. *Calle Castelar 64–66.* ☎ *787/742-0090.*

www.mamacitasguesthouse.com. Reservations not required. Lunch main courses $6.50–$10; dinner main courses $12–$22. MC, V. Breakfast, lunch & dinner daily. Map p 128.

Where to **Stay**

Casa Ensenada Waterfront Guesthouse DEWEY   A low-key spot with clean and comfortable rooms and a great patio for sunbathing and nighttime barbecues. You can take a kayak to the Dinghy Dock restaurant. There's also a library, snorkeling gear, a kitchenette, and coffeemaker. *Calle Escudero 142.* ☎ *866/210-0704 or 787/742-3559. www.casaensenada.com. 3 units. Doubles $85–$175. MC, V. Map p 128.*

Club Seabourne CULEBRA Overlooking Fulladosa Bay, the club's dining room serves some of the best food on Culebra, with fresh lobster, shrimp, snapper, grouper, and conch, as well as steaks. The hotel also has a patio bar with a nightly happy hour, plus one of two pools on the island. It's down a country road from town in a lush setting. *Fulladosa Rd. (P.O. Box 357).* ☎ *787/742-3169. www.clubseabourne.com. 12 units. Doubles $165–$219. Rates include breakfast. AE, MC, V. From Dewey (Puebla), follow Fulladosa Rd. along the south side of the bay for 1½ miles (2.4km). Map p 128.*

Posada la Hamaca CULEBRA This was one of Culebra's original guesthouses, lying in town next to the Dewey Bridge. Although it has competition, the place is still going strong. Simply furnished accommodations are well

maintained and tidily kept, each with a private bathroom. Beach towels, coolers, and free ice are provided for beach outings. Some units are large enough to accommodate four guests, making them suitable for families. One apartment is spacious enough to accommodate 8 to 12 guests. *Calle Castellar 68.* ☎ *787/742-3516. www.posada. com. 10 units. Doubles $97, apt $134–$190. MC, V. Map p 128.*

★ **Tamarindo Estates** CULEBRA Set on 60 lush acres (24 hectares) along a private bay, this beachfront resort offers rooms in laid-back, kitchen-equipped cottages. A bar-cafe is on a roof deck beside the pool. The cottages are screened and have fans. *Tamarindo Beach Rd.* ☎ *787/742-3343. www.tamarindo estates.com. 12 cottages. Doubles $140–$190. AE, MC, V. Map p 128.*

Villa Boheme DEWEY   This modest guesthouse opens onto views of Ensenada Bay, and its hosts invite you to explore their little island by kayak or bike. Out back is a great terrace with hammocks that invite you to lead the life of leisure. The best units are a trio of large efficiencies. *Calle Fulladosa 368.* ☎ *787/ 742-3508. www.villaboheme.com. 11 units. Doubles $107–$152. AE, MC, V. Map p 128.* ●

The Best Beaches

Beaches Best Bets

Boquerón Beach 16

Caña Gorda 15

Carolina Public Beach 8

Condado Beach 4

Crash Boat 2

El Convento Beach 10

Seven Seas Public Beach 11

Flamenco Beach 12

Isla Verde 6

Jobos Beach 3

Best for **White Sand**
★★ Flamenco Beach, *Rte. 250/251
to Calle Ecudero, Culebra (p 137)*

Best for **Body Surfing**
★ Condado Beach, *near Calle Taft
at Av. Ashford, Condado, San Juan
(p 136)*

Best for **Solitude**
★★★ El Convento Beach, *Hwy. 30,
Fajardo (p 136)*

Best for **Families**
★ Luquillo Beach, *Hwy. 3, Luquillo
(p 137)*

Best for **Picnicking**
Carolina Public Beach, *Rte. 187,
Carolina (p 136)*

Best for **Romance**
★ Isla Verde, *Av. Isla Verde, from
Punta Las Marias to Calle Violeta,
San Juan (p 137)*

Best for **People-Watching**
★ Condado, *along Av. Ashford,
from the Puente de Dos Hermanos
Bridge to Calle Taft, San Juan (p 136)*

Best for **Swimming**
★★ Pine Grove Beach, *Isla Verde,
San Juan (p 138)*

Best for **Shade**
★★ Boquerón Beach, *Boquerón,
Rte. 101 ends at the beach entrance,
Cabo Rojo (p 136)*

Best for **Snorkeling**
★★ Media Luna Beach, *Rte. 996 to
Sun Bay Beach, Vieques (p 137)*

Best for **Board Surfing**
★★ Jobos Beach, *Rte. 466, Isabela
(p 137)*

Best **View**
★★★ Zoni Beach, *Rte. 250/251 to
Calle B, Culebra (p 138)*

Previous page: Surfing on Crash Boat Beach.

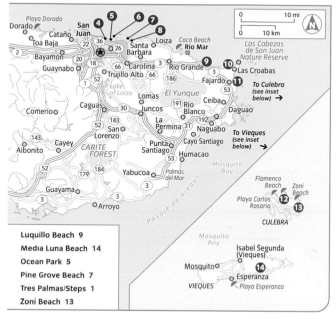

Luquillo Beach 9
Media Luna Beach 14
Ocean Park 5
Pine Grove Beach 7
Tres Palmas/Steps 1
Zoni Beach 13

Best for **Windsurfing/
Kite-sailing**
★★ Ocean Park, *Hwy. 36, San Juan*
(p 137)

Best for **Sunbathing**
★★ Caña Gorda, *Rte. 333, Guánica*
(p 136)

Crash Boat Beach.

Puerto Rico **Beaches A to Z**

★★ **Boquerón Beach** This fine public beach and adjacent village brings to mind a tropical Cape Cod. The 3-mile (4.8km) beach arcs in a wide, white-sand beach lined with palm trees and fat sea-grape bushes; its calm water is perfect for swimming and snorkeling. With showers and changing areas, bathrooms, a snack bar and sundry shop, along with barbecue and shaded picnic areas, the beach is perfect for families. It's easy to walk to the adjacent village, a colorful strip of open-air, wooden and cement establishments along the waterfront selling seafood fritters and ice-cold drinks. *Boquerón, Cabo Rojo.*

★★ **Caña Gorda** Floating on your back is a snap here due to the water's high salt content; the buoyancy of the water makes it a great spot to teach kids to swim. You take a winding country road over a mountainside that offers breathtaking views as it drops back down to the coast. This pretty and often uncrowded (except weekends) beach is right beside the Guánica Dry Forest nature reserve and bird sanctuary. You can continue past the public beach area and find your own isolated spot farther along the road. *Km 6.4 Rte. 333, Guánica.*

Carolina Public Beach This wide public beach, bordered by tropical pine forest, has some of the best surf and sand in the San Juan metro area, plus the convenience of lockers, outdoor showers, restrooms, and easy parking. It's a bit far out, however, if you don't have a car (btw Isla Verde and Piñones), but you can walk here easily from the Ritz-Carlton or Marriott Courtyard Isla Verde hotels along adjacent Pine Grove Beach. *Just east of the Marriott Courtyard Isla Verde Hotel,* *along Rte. 187, on the road to Piñones, Carolina.*

★ **Condado Beach** Tourists and local fashionistas congregate by the beach in front of La Concha with local youths, while farther east in front of the Atlantic Beach Hotel is the place to be if you are beautiful and gay. Families congregate near the little beach by the protected entrance to the Condado Lagoon cove and in front of the Marriott; and surfers flock farther east by Ashford Presbyterian Hospital.

Locals prefer the area around Parque del Indio, where the beach is wider and a grove of towering palm trees lessens the glint from the condominiums. *The beach runs along Av. Ashford, from the Puente de Dos Hermanos Bridge to Calle Taft just beyond Parque del Indio, San Juan.*

Crash Boat This postcard-perfect beach is used by families, fishermen, and surfers. Modest shacks nearby sell seafood, snacks, and cold drinks. Part of the beach is sheltered from the open ocean and is great for kids; the other side gets strong surf and is preferred by surfers. *From Hwy. 2, Rte. 107 runs through town & to the north, where the beach is located, Isabela.*

★★★ **El Convento Beach** About 7 miles (11km) of undeveloped coastline stretches from Fajardo to Luquillo. A rustic wooden cottage is maintained for Puerto Rico's governor and official guests, but it's the only development on the coast, a nesting site for endangered sea turtles and an outstanding snorkeling site. It's a 2-mile (3.2km) hike from the **Seven Seas Public Beach.** *Take Av. El Conquistador to Cabesas Hwy., which passes the public beach* on its way to Las Croabas fishing village, Fajardo.

★★ Flamenco Beach Quite simply one of the most picturesque—and most photographed—beaches in the Caribbean. This mile-long beach has some of the silkiest, whitest sand anywhere, and it stretches languidly across a horseshoe-shaped cove fronting remarkably blue water. *From Dewey take Rte. 250/251 to Calle Ecudero, Culebra.*

★ Isla Verde This wide, golden beach is lined with luxury hotels and condos. The beach draws beautiful crowds of sunbathers, swimmers, and watersports enthusiasts who can do it all, from parasailing to renting a catamaran. Beachfront hotels host the city's best restaurants, nightclubs, and bars. The beach itself has a party vibe, especially on weekends. *Av. Isla Verde, from Punta Las Marias to Calle Violeta, San Juan.*

★★ Jobos Beach The famed surf break at this Isabela beach is among the island's best, but this spot made the grade because of its huge swath of sand with a sheltered area for kids. It's in the island's quintessential surf town, complete with seafood restaurants and bars, funky guesthouses, and frequent outdoor

live music. *Take Rte. 466 from Hwy. 2 north to the coast, Isabela.*

★ Luquillo Beach This crescent bay's emerald waters are shielded by a coral reef and bordered by a wide beach backed by a coconut grove and mountains. The facilities (picnic areas, showers and changing rooms, bathrooms, and snack bars) are kept in tip-top shape. *30 miles (48km) east of San Juan along Rte. 3, Luquillo.*

★★ Media Luna Beach You take a jutted dirt road from Sun Bay on Vieques's south coast to get to this hidden beach, which is protected by reefs and fronted by palm trees. The snorkeling is easy and rewarding. Though it feels isolated, it's very accessible, close to the tourist village of Esperanza and right beside Sun and Mosquito bays. *From Rte. 996, enter the Sun Bay public beach area but follow the dirt road beyond it, Vieques.*

★★ Ocean Park This wide beach, lined with palm and sea-grape trees, fronts a residential neighborhood of beautiful homes. Young and beautiful *sanjuaneros* congregate here; it's a popular spot to swim, play paddle tennis, and kite surf. Upscale guesthouses, most with good restaurants open to the public, attract urbane visitors from the East Coast. The

Flamenco Beach.

Pine Grove Beach.

beach ends at Ultimo Trolley, the beach in front of Barbosa Park, with track and field, baseball, basketball, and tennis courts. Musicians perform on weekends, and the many food vendors make this a great stop for a snack and drink. *The beach runs east of Calle Taft beyond Ultimo Trolley to where the beach ends at Punta Las Marias, San Juan.*

★★ **Pine Grove Beach** This crescent, white-sand beach's tranquil, rich blue waters are protected by an offshore reef from the often rough Atlantic current, making it a perfect spot to learn to surf. A long sandbar and calm, shallow water stretch far offshore near the Ritz-Carlton and the Casa Cuba social club to the west. There's more surf to the east, which is a popular spot for surfing, boogie-boarding, and bodysurfing. Lessons and rentals are available. *The beach stretches btw the Ritz-Carlton & the Marriott Courtyard hotels at the end of Isla Verde near the airport, San Juan.*

Tres Palmas/Steps Of all the spots along Rincón's 8 miles (13km) of beachfront—Puntas, Domes, Las Marías, and the Spanish Wall—this bit of coast can deliver the full Rincón experience. Depending on the season, or its mood, you'll either get some of the famed Puerto Rico pipeline's most powerful waves, or clear, tropical waters with gorgeous reefs and marine life just off the beach. It's beautiful all the time, and the adjacent beaches are a natural marine reserve. *Near the intersection of Rte. 413 & La Joya, Rincón.*

★★★ **Zoni Beach** I once found a message in a bottle here, left months before after a wild New Year's Party on one of the French Caribbean islands. It seemed perfectly natural on this stretch of sand, which feels like a slice of paradise at the end of the world. This beautiful, isolated spot is more than 5 miles (8km) from Dewey and is set off by scrub forest and has beautiful waters, rife with tropical fish and reefs. The snorkeling is fine, and so is finding this beach all to yourself, an increasing difficulty. There's nothing but brilliantly blue sky and sea surrounding the spot. *Rte. 250/251 to Calle B; turn left & take until the end, Culebra.* ●

7 The Great Outdoors

El Yunque National Forest

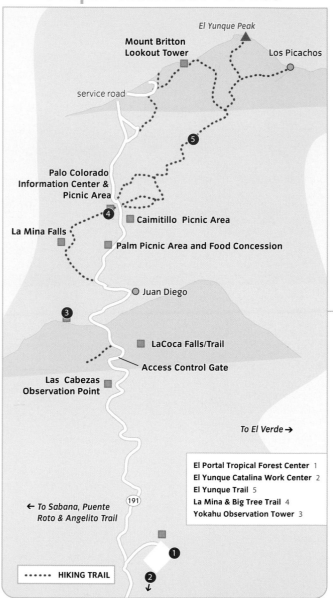

El Yunque Peak

Mount Britton Lookout Tower

Los Picachos

service road

Palo Colorado Information Center & Picnic Area

4

5

Caimitillo Picnic Area

La Mina Falls

Palm Picnic Area and Food Concession

Juan Diego

3

LaCoca Falls/Trail

Access Control Gate

Las Cabezas Observation Point

To El Verde →

El Portal Tropical Forest Center	1
El Yunque Catalina Work Center	2
El Yunque Trail	5
La Mina & Big Tree Trail	4
Yokahu Observation Tower	3

← To Sabana, Puente Roto & Angelito Trail

(191)

1

······ HIKING TRAIL

2
↓

Previous page: Trail in El Yunque.

This lush, mystical rainforest has evoked a feeling of reverence in island residents for centuries. Its name comes from the Taíno word for the god worshipped by Puerto Rico's ancient residents for protecting the island from hurricanes and other calamities from his lair in the misty green mountains of the rainforest.

The forest sprawls across a 28,000-acre (11,200-hectare) preserve in the Sierra Luquillo Mountains, with its highest peak, El Toro, often cloud capped, overlooking the island's beautiful northeast coast. Originally granted its national forest reserve status when President Theodore Roosevelt created the national parks system, the forest remains in a virgin state. It's home to hundreds of different tree and tropical plant species, with 150 types of ferns and 50 types of orchids alone. Hundreds of different animals live here, including 68 bird species, like the endangered and elusive bright-green Puerto Rican parrot, which was once near extinction but is making a comeback.

Some 100 billion gallons of rain fall here annually, and the reserve is run through with cold mountain streams and rivers, like the Río Espirtu Santo, the Holy Spirit River, the island's most powerful, which tumbles down from the rainforest highlands, through bamboo and mangrove forest, to the coast and then out to the Atlantic Ocean. The river becomes navigable below El Yunque, and though at some points it's less than 5 feet (1.5m) deep, there are spots where it is said to plunge 50 feet (15m). Kayaks are the best bet for navigating it, as the ride out to the Atlantic does require walking in a few spots.

❶ El Portal Tropical Forest Center. This state-of-the-art center on Rte. 191 in Río Grande (☎ 787/888-1880) has 10,000 square feet (929 sq. m) of exhibition space and provides a thorough overview of the rainforest in three different pavilions with bilingual displays. Famous Puerto Ricans narrate documentaries about the forest that are shown here. *Open daily, 9am to 5pm. Admission $3 adults, $1.50 for children under 12.*

❷ The El Yunque Catalina Work Center. Beside the main highway at the forest's northern edge (☎ 787/888-1880), the center has useful information on hiking and camping. Group tours are available,

El Portal Tropical Forest Center.

Tropical foliage.

main road, they can be appreciated with minimal physical exertion. Right after Rte. 191 enters the reserve, you'll pass a lookout spot near a souvenir stand, which is worth a look. The main attraction, **La Coca Falls,** is located at Km 8.2. Cold mountain water barrels hundreds of feet down into a pool beside the roadway, wearing down the mountainside and the boulders until they're smooth and green.

❸ Farther along is the **Yokahu Observation Tower,** a circular stone watchtower that has a circular stairway leading to a rooftop observation point. There's a wonderful view of untarnished northeastern coast, with the sunbleached beaches of Luquillo and beyond, glaring through perforations in the lush, green canopy at the base of the tower.

❹ **La Mina & Big Tree Trail.** Truly exploring what El Yunque has to offer requires both time a bit of effort. The best bet for most visitors is La Mina and Big Tree Trail, which takes 2 hours round-trip. It's a beautiful walk from a parking area right along Rte. 191. The trail descends along La Mina River, which

but reservations must be arranged in advance. The 2-hour tours are conducted Saturday to Monday every hour on the hour from 10:30am to 3:30pm; they cost $5 for adults and $3 for children under 12. Because most of El Yunque's major attractions can be seen from the

La Mina Falls.

Travel Tips

From San Juan, take Rte. 26 or the Baldorioty de Castro Expressway East to Carolina, where you will pick up Rte. 66 or the Roberto Sánchez Vilella Expressway. The $1.50 toll road will take you farther along Rte. 3, putting you in Canóvanas. Go right (east) on Rte. 3, which you follow east to the intersection of Rte. 191, a two-lane highway that heads south into the forest. Take 191 for 3 miles (4.8km), going through the village of Palmer. As the road rises, you will enter the El Yunque National Forest.

The El Portal Tropical Forest Center is right inside the reserve. Although the center is educational, if you are pressed for time, forgo it and head straight to the rainforest's major attractions; many are easily accessible from the main road, and maps, brochures, and signage throughout the park make exploring on your own a breeze. Dress in shorts or a bathing suit and good walking shoes, and bring a poncho or umbrella—this is a rainforest, after all. One of the forest's biggest pleasures is taking a dip in the mountain streams, so plan to get wet. The beautiful Luquillo Beach is a 10-minute drive from the base of the rainforest, so visitors often pair up a morning trek in the rainforest with an afternoon at the public beach, which has full facilities. A good meal can be had at the adjacent food kiosks right next to the public beach.

transforms from a trickle, to a stream, to a raging torrent. Along the way, you'll pass through lush forest, with informational displays explaining the surroundings at interspersed points of interest along the way. It ends at La Mina Falls, which crash into a natural pool. It's a delicious swim, freezing at first but very refreshing. Beyond the falls, the Big Tree Trail climbs up through a forested area, which is home to native birds, like the screech owl and the bullfinch.

5 El Yunque Trail. This 2-hour hike to the rainforest's upper peaks is the most challenging, in parts a steep, winding path. You will pass through the different forest types—sierra palm and Palo Colorado and then upward into the cloud-covered Mt. Britton dwarf forest. Lookout peaks include **Yunque Rock,** and **Los Picachos,** and you can see out to the Atlantic and Caribbean on clear days. The trail begins at El Caimitillo Picnic Grounds.

Other Natural Wonders

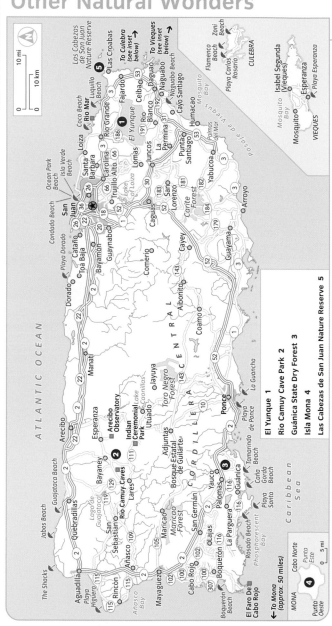

El Yunque **1**

Rio Camuy Cave Park **2**

Guánica State Dry Forest **3**

Isla Mona **4**

Las Cabezas de San Juan Nature Reserve **5**

ATLANTIC OCEAN

Caribbean Sea

CORDILLERA CENTRAL

CULEBRA

VIEQUES

MONA

esides El Yunque, Puerto Rico has more than 20 other forest reserves and stunning natural wonders. Below are some highlights.

Parque de las Cavernas del Río Camuy (Río Camuy Cave Park).

This wondrous park contains the third-largest underground river in the world and provides the opportunity to peer into what is a vast underground world: miles of underground rivers twisting through a network of caves, canyons, and sinkholes that have been cut through the island's limestone base over the course of millions of years. You need at least 2 hours for an adequate experience, but the more adventurous can take full-day tours exploring a part of the mysterious world with private tour operators. The caves have been known by locals since the time of the Taínos, but were first officially explored by speleologists in 1958 after being led there by local boys. Today, visitors explore most sites via the park trolley: a 200-foot-deep (60m) sinkhole; a chasm containing a tropical forest, complete with birds and butterflies and a huge waterfall; and the entrance of Cueva Clare, the park's premier cave, a 45-minute odyssey through a fascinating underworld of stalactites and sculpted cavern walls. Tres Pueblos Sinkhole is 65 feet (20m) wide and 400 feet (120m) deep; it's named for its location at the border of the towns of Camuy, Hatillo, and Lares. *Located north at Km 2 on Rte. 129 from Rte. 111. ☎ 787/898-3100. Wed–Sun 8am–4pm. Admission $12 adults, $7 children 4–12 & $5 for seniors. Parking $2.*

Guánica State Dry Forest.

This bonsai-like forest sprawled across an astonishing section of southeast coastline and the headlands overlooking it was declared a World Biosphere Reserve by the United Nations. The subtropical ecosystem is home to 750 plants and tree species and half the island bird species,

Río Camuy Cave Park.

Bird-watching in Guánica State Dry Forest.

including the endangered Puerto Rican nightjar, as well as a number of different migratory birds. The park is ruggedly beautiful; make sure to visit the beaches along Rte. 333. It's a good hike from the main parking area. You can take a car by backtracking to Rte. 116. You'll have to drive back through the main entrance, turn left on Rte. 116, and then turn left on Rte. 333, which climbs a gorgeous mountain pass overlooking Guánica Bay and the gorgeous southwest coast. Just continue straight beyond the Copamarina Beach Resort to get to the back

Isla Mona.

end of the forest and the beaches bordering it.

The ranger station next to the main parking lot has good information about hiking trails. Heckle the staff (if anyone is around) for a Xeroxed copy of the reserve's trail guide, which outlines 36 miles (58km) of trails through the four forest types. The most interesting is the mile-long (1.6km) **Cueva Trail,** which gives you the most scenic look at the various types of vegetation. To reach the heart of the forest, take Rte. 334 from Rte. 116, right before the main town of Guánica. You can explore it from the coast along Rte. 333, too.

Isla Mona. Adrift in the ferocious Mona Passage, halfway between Puerto Rico and the Dominican Republic, this isolated island has been left alone by modern man, save for the occasional smuggler or illegal immigrant, and is known as the Caribbean Galápagos because it teems with giant iguanas, endangered sea turtles, and huge seabirds. Its shores rise up in steep, 200-foothigh (60m) limestone cliffs, and the ocean surrounding it has huge coral reefs and undersea caves, which are home to an incredible array of sea life. There are also miles of secluded

Experiencing "Burning Water"

One of Puerto Rico's biggest wonders is that it is home to three bioluminescent bays, one at Las Cabezas de San Juan Nature Reserve, one across the bay in Vieques, and one in the southeast in La Parguera. The best is Vieques's Mosquito Bay, followed by Fajardo's lagoon, and then La Parguera, which has been dimmed by pollution. Tiny bioluminescent organisms leave bluish-white trails of phosphorescence when disturbed, illuminating the water at night, especially in the absence of other lights; as such, it's best on moonless nights. On Vieques, **Island Adventures** (☎ 787/741-0720) and **Blue Caribe Kayak** (☎ 787/741-2522 for details) run trips for about $35 per person. In Fajardo, Gary Horne's *Las Tortugas Adventures* (P.O. Box 1637, Canovanas; ☎ 787/809-0253 or 787/637-8356) is next to the harbor at Las Croabas, along with a number of other reputable operators giving kayak tours. The kayak trip across the bay and through mangrove canals is as much a part of the adventure as seeing the biobay, which is beautiful. Appreciation of it is dimmed, however, by ambient light in the area.

white-sand beaches and palm-tree groves. Though largely uninhabited today, it was home to Taíno settlements. Pirates (including Capt. Kidd) used it as a hideout and a base for raids. It also attracted the famous and powerful, with both Columbus and Ponce de León stopping here. With no fresh water or other amenities, a trip here is for the hardy. Mona can be reached by organized tour from Mayagüez. Camping is available at $10 per night. Everything needed, including water, must be brought in, and everything must also be taken out. For more information, call the **Puerto Rico Department of Natural and Environmental Resources** at ☎ 787/999-2200. The Puerto Rico government invested $1.7 million on a new visitor center on Mona, which includes living quarters for researchers and park rangers. *To reach the island, contact Adventures Tourmarine, Rte. 102 Km 14.1, Playa Joyuda, Cabo Rojo (☎ 787/375-2625; www.tourmarine pr.com) or Acampa Nature Adventures (Av. Piñero 1221, San Juan 00902; ☎ 787/706-0659; www. acampapr.com).*

Las Cabezas de San Juan Nature Reserve is surrounded on three sides by ocean and sprawls across 316 acres (126 hectares) of scrub forest, lagoons, silky sand beaches, cliffs, offshore cays, and coral reefs. Boardwalk trails wind through mangrove coastal forests. There are seven distinct ecological systems and a restored 19th-century Spanish colonial lighthouse, which affords views all the way out to the U.S. Virgin Islands. The nature reserve is open Wednesday through Sunday. *Rte. 987 Km 6, Fajardo. Reservations required; call ☎ 787/722-5882 (weekdays) or ☎ 787/860-2560 (weekends). Admission $7 for adults, $4 for children under 13, and $2.50 for seniors. Guided 2½-hr. tours are conducted at 9:30, 10, and 10:30am, and 2pm (in English at 2pm).*

Puerto Rico's Best Golf Courses

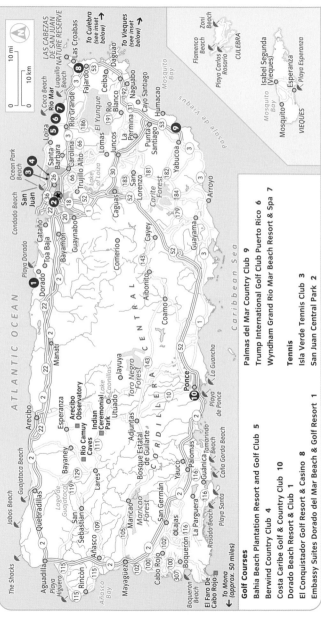

Golf Courses

Bahia Beach Plantation Resort and Golf Club **5**

Berwind Country Club **4**

Costa Caribe Golf & Country Club **10**

Dorado Beach Resort & Club **1**

El Conquistador Golf Resort & Casino **8**

Embassy Suites Dorado del Mar Beach & Golf Resort **1**

Palmas del Mar Country Club **9**

Trump International Golf Club Puerto Rico **6**

Wyndham Grand Rio Mar Beach Resort & Spa **7**

Tennis

Isla Verde Tennis Club **3**

San Juan Central Park **2**

With nearly 30 golf courses, Puerto Rico stakes claim as the Scotland of the Caribbean, with designs by Puerto Rico's own Chi Chi Rodriguez, Greg Norman, George and Tom Fazio, Jack Nicklaus, Arthur Hills, and Robert Trent Jones and sons.

It would take weeks to golf all the courses that are worth a look on the island, with dramatic coastal runways and intriguing jungle and river greens serving as recurring motifs. The Puerto Rico Open at the Trump property in Río Grande is getting a lot of attention, both as a successful local event and an annual tournament that could be poised to grow in prominence on the PGA Tour.

★ **Bahia Beach Plantation Resort and Golf Club.** Robert Trent Jones, Jr.'s 2008 renovation sprawls across 480 acres (192 hectares) of beachfront and adjacent green valley in the shadow of El Yunque and along the Espiritu Santo River. The new course joins those built by other members of the Jones family. Dad Trent Jones, Sr. built the legendary Dorado Beach East golf course, and brother Reese Jones completed Palmas del Mar's Flamboyán course in 1999. A St. Regis resort is underway. Greens fees are $225 weekdays, $275 weekends. *Rte. 187 Km 4.2.* ☎ *787/857-5800. www.bahiabeachpuertorico.com.*

Berwind Country Club. Built on a former coconut plantation with ocean views, towering palms, and frenzied tropical foliage, this is the nearest full-size course to San Juan. The course is challenging, with water hazards and three tough closing holes. Greens fees are $65. *Loiza, Rte. 187 Km 4.7.* ☎ *787/876-5380.*

Costa Caribe Golf & Country Club. The 27-hole course, conceived as three distinct 9s, spreads out on former sugarcane fields with commanding views of the ocean and mountains. Players are charged for 18 holes and can play them in any combination of the 9s. Greens fees are a reasonable $85 ($75 for guests), including golf carts. *At the Ponce Hilton Golf & Casino Resort, Av. Caribe 1150 (P.O. Box 7419), Ponce.* ☎ *787/848-1000 or 787/812-2650. www.costacaribe-resort.com.*

Bahia Beach Golf Club.

Dorado Beach Resort & Club.

Dorado Beach is home to four legendary championship golf courses. The East and West Courses, originally designed by Robert Trent Jones, Sr., are spread along two miles of Puerto Rico's northeasterly shores within the former Rockefeller estate's magnificent, mature landscaping. These two courses run through lush jungle and oceanfront coconut groves and are known for their tight fairways, and for the East Course's famed 4th hole ending at the water's edge. The two newer Plantation courses offer wide-open fairways, large bunkers, water hazards, and beautiful mountain views. The East Course is scheduled for renovation in 2010, followed by the West Course, both under the watchful eye of Robert Trent Jones, Jr., to ensure the renovations remain faithful to his father's original designs. Greens fees average $160. *Dorado Beach Resort & Club, 100 Dorado Beach Dr., Ste. 1, Dorado.* ☎ *787/796-1234.*

El Conquistador Golf Resort & Casino.

The Arthur Hills Golf Course at El Conquistador Resort was rightly named one of the Best Places to Play 2008/2009 by *Golf Digest.* With its challenging, hilly terrain, this course demands precision from players, but

Dorado Beach Resort & Club.

also rewards them with fantastic mountain and sea views. The resort also has numerous activities to occupy non-golfers. Greens fees $180. *1000 El Conquistador Ave., Las Croabas.* ☎ *787/863-6784.*

Embassy Suites Dorado del Mar Beach & Golf Resort.

Chi Chi Rodriguez's signature par-72, 18-hole golf course is set against a panoramic backdrop of mountains and ocean. Greens fees start at $120. *Dorado del Mar Blvd. 210, Dorado.* ☎ *787/796-6125. www.embassy suitesdorado.com.*

★★ Palmas del Mar Country Club.

Two courses, one designed by Gary Player and the other by Reese Jones, are on offer here. Greens fees are $85 guests, $100 for nonguests. *At Palmas del Mar resort community, Hwy. 3 Km 86.4, Humacao.* ☎ *787/285-2256. www.palmas countryclub.com.*

★ Trump International Golf Club Puerto Rico.

The home of the new Puerto Rico Open PGA Tour Event marks the extension of the Trump brand to Puerto Rico, which Donald Trump announced as a $600-million investment with local partner Arturo Diaz to construct luxury

El Conquistador Golf Resort.

vacation villas and make other improvements in 2008. Part of that was invested in bringing the course up to PGA specs to make the PR Open a reality. It's now two beautiful courses, which run along ocean coast, lake shores and highlands, and lush jungle settings. It wins raves from both pros and weekend warriors. Greens fees range from $140 to $160 for visitors. *100 Clubhouse Dr., Río Grande. ☎ 787/657-2000. www.trumpgolfclubpuertorico.com.*

Wyndham Grand Rio Mar Beach Resort & Spa.
Wyndham has two world-class courses stretching out in the shadow of El Yunque along a dazzling stretch of coast: There's Tom and George Fazio's 6,782-yard (6,104m) oceanfront course and Greg Norman's 6,945-yard (6,251m) romp along a lush

Trump International Golf Club Puerto Rico.

jungle river. Greens fees are $165 for guests and $200 for nonresident walk-ons. *Río Mar Blvd., Río Grande. ☎ 787/636-0636. www.wyndham riomar.com.*

Tennis

Puerto Rico has about 100 tennis courts spread among hotels and resorts, even some smaller inns, and at public parks throughout the island. Most of the big resorts have their own tennis courts for the use of guests and other visitors. Palmas del Mar, El Conquistador, and Río Mar are all known for their tennis facilities, which feature Har-Tru and other quality courts.

San Juan Central Park is an impressively maintained public park with 20 tennis courts and four racquetball courts, all well maintained and recently renovated. There are also track-and-field facilities, a children's playground, an indoor Olympic pool and diving tank, and a jogging path. Tennis fees are $3 per hour from 6am to 5pm, and $4 per hour from 6 to 10pm. There is also a $1 per vehicle entrance charge. *Calle Cerra exit from Av. Muñoz Rivera, or Av. Kennedy (Hwy. 2; ☎ 787/722-1646). Open daily.*

Isla Verde Tennis Club is open all week: Monday to Friday 8am to10pm, Saturday 8am to 7pm, and Sunday from 8am to 6pm. Courts cost from $15 to $20 an hour. There are four plexipave hard courts and a hitting wall, with night lighting. *Corner of Calles Palmera and Rodríguez Ema (behind Mundo Feliz Condo), Urb. Palmera Sur, Isla Verde. ☎ 787/727-6490.*

Adventures in the Ocean

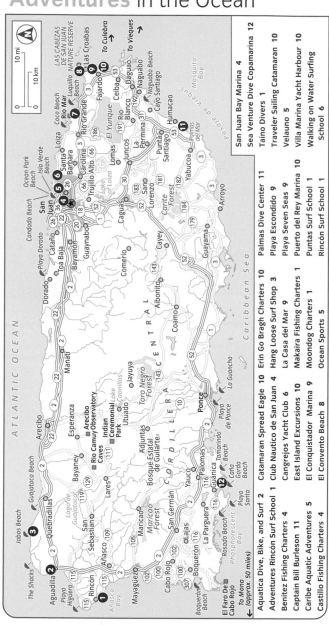

Aquatica Dive, Bike, and Surf **2**
Adventures Rincón Surf School **1**
Benitez Fishing Charters **4**
Captain Bill Burleson **11**
Caribe Aquatic Adventures **5**
Castillo Fishing Charters **4**
Catamaran Spread Eagle **10**
Club Nautico de San Juan **1**
Cangrejos Yacht Club **6**
East Island Excursions **10**
El Conquistador Marina **9**
El Convento Beach **8**
Erin Go Bragh Charters **11**
Hang Loose Surf Shop **3**
La Casa del Mar **9**
Makaira Fishing Charters **1**
Moondog Charters **1**
Ocean Sports **5**
Palmas Dive Center **11**
Playa Escondido **9**
Playa Seven Seas **9**
Puerto del Rey Marina **10**
Puntas Surf School **1**
Rincón Surf School **1**
San Juan Bay Marina **4**
Sea Venture Dive Copamarina **12**
Taino Divers **1**
Traveler Sailing Catamaran **10**
Velauno **5**
Villa Marina Yacht Harbour **10**
Walking on Water Surfing
School **6**

With its warm, gin-clear waters, countless reefs and islands, and unique position on the edge of the continental shelf, Puerto Rico is a paradise for the aquatically inclined.

Snorkeling

Snorkeling is better in the outlying portions of the island than in San Juan. Day trips with transportation from San Juan are available for around $100 per person. Inquire at your hotel desk about operators.

Some of the best snorkeling in Puerto Rico is in and around Fajardo. Its public beach, **Playa Seven Seas,** is an attractive and sheltered strip of sand. The beach lies on the southwestern shoreline of Las Cabezas peninsula and is crowded on weekends. You can swim out to the reef a hundred yards offshore to see small, colorful fish and marine plant life. For even better snorkeling, walk to the western end of this beach and along a dirt path cutting through a wooded mount. After about a half mile (.8km), you'll come to another path heading to **Playa Escondido (Hidden Beach),** a small, white-sand cove with coral reefs in aquamarine waters right off this beach. If you continue straight for another mile, you will come to the gorgeous **El Convento Beach,** stretching out along the miles-long undeveloped coastline between Fajardo and Luquillo. Just offshore, the ocean floor drops to depths of 15 feet (4.5m) and the water is choked with reefs, small tropical fish, and larger species as well. This is all in the shadow of El Yunque and a pristine, white, sandy beach. Several operators offer day trips (10am–3pm) from Fajardo's marinas that include sailing, snorkeling, swimming, and a stop at one of the island beaches, where lunch is usually served. It's the easiest way to really experience the Caribbean marine world while in Puerto Rico. Prices, including lunch and equipment, start from about $70 per person. The trips are aboard luxury catamarans, with plush seating, sound systems, and other comforts, like a bar. Captains know the best spots, where reefs attract schools of feeding fish, depending on conditions. These are among the most gin-clear and tranquil waters in Puerto Rico. They teem with wildlife, including several species of fish

Snorkeling.

Snorkeling.

such as grouper, but also lobster, moray eels, and sea turtles. Among the local operators are **Traveler Sailing Catamaran** (☎ 787/853-2821), **East Island Excursions** (☎ 787/860-3434), and **Catamaran Spread Eagle** (☎ 787/887-8821. **Erin Go Bragh Charters** (☎ 787/860-4401) offers similar day trips aboard a 50-foot (15m) sailing ketch.

Boating/Sailing

San Juan has three marinas. The **San Juan Bay Marina** (☎ 787/721-8062) and **Club Nautico de San Juan** (☎ 787/722-0177) are adjacent to the Condado bridge and the Convention Center district in Miramar. The other marina, the **Cangrejos Yacht Club** (Rte. 187, Piñones; ☎ 787/791-1015), is at the border of Isla Verde and Piñones near the airport. There is no greater proof of Fajardo's fame as a sailor's paradise than its seven marinas. The most renowned is the **Puerto del Rey Marina** (Rte. 3 Km 51.4; ☎ 787/860-1000 or 787/801-3010). The swankiest marina in Fajardo, it's a beautiful 1,100-slip facility south of town, the largest in the Caribbean. It's like a city unto itself with restaurants, bars, and a host of

other services. **Villa Marina Yacht Harbour** (Rte. 987 Km 1.3; ☎ 787/863-5131 or 787/863-5011) is the other main marina in town, and is the shortest ride to the offshore cays and isolated white-sand beaches on the mainland. Charters operate out of both. There's a private 35-slip marina at the lowest level of the **El Conquistador** (☎ 787/863-1000).

Fishing

Big-game fish are found close to shore across Puerto Rico, so you won't waste time traveling to fishing spots. You can leave in the early morning; make it to the grounds of the allison tuna, white and blue marlin, sailfish, wahoo, and dolphin or mahimahi (known locally as dorado); bag a big game fish; and be back at the marina by early afternoon. Some 30 world records have been broken in island waters. Half-day deep-sea fishing trips (4 hours) start at around $550, whereas full-day charters begin at around $900. Most charters hold six passengers in addition to the crew. Although fishing is good year round, the winter season from October to early March is the best. Blue marlin can be caught all summer and into the fall, and renowned big game fish tournaments take place in August and September.

Benitez Fishing Charters offers trips aboard the plush and comfortable *Sea Born,* a 45-foot (13.5m) air-conditioned deluxe Hatteras yacht. Half-day tours cost $642; full-day tours are $1,017. *Club Nautico, Miramar.* ☎ 787/723-2292.

Castillo Fishing Charters has been running charters out of the marina since 1975. Captain Joe Castillo runs the company with his son, José Iván, and daughter, Vanessa, and they know their stuff. The

Legend, a 48-foot (14m) Hatteras, is an excellent vessel built for fishing and comfort. Half-day tours cost $700; full days are $1,100. *San Juan Bay Marina, Miramar.* ☎ *787/726-5752.*

Captain Bill Burleson offers fishing trips aboard a 46-foot (14m) sport-fishing craft. He's a seasoned pro who knows the hot spots off Puerto Rico's east coast. Burleson prefers to take fishing groups to Grappler Banks, 18 nautical miles (33km) away, which lie in the migratory paths of wahoo, tuna, and marlin. A maximum of six people are taken out, costing $800 for 4½ hours, $960 for 6 hours, or $1,280 for 8 hours. Burleson also offers snorkeling charter expeditions starting at $640 for up to 6 persons. *Based in Palmas del Mar, Humacao.* ☎ *787/850-7442.*

Makaira Fishing Charters (☎ 787/823-4391 or 787/299-7374) and **Moondog Charters** (☎ 787/823-3059) are both good bets for charters out of Rincón.

Scuba Diving

The continental shelf surrounding Puerto Rico on three sides is rife with coral reefs, caves, sea walls, and trenches. From the large canyon off the south coast to Mona Island and the unnamed cays off the main island's east coast, Puerto Rico is full of top-notch dive sites. Introductory courses for beginners are generally between $90 and $130; two-tank dives for experienced divers run up to $150.

Caribe Aquatic Adventures. This outfitter runs scuba and snorkeling trips in the San Juan metro area and off the east coast. One-hour snorkel tours are $50; a resort scuba course is $130. *Calle 19 1062, Villa Nevarez, San Juan.* ☎ *787/281-8858. Daily 9am–9pm.*

Ocean Sports. Ocean Sports runs diving courses and scuba and snorkeling trips out of its San Juan office. It also rents kayaks. Dives cost $125; the resort course is $125. *Main office Av. Isla Verde 77, Isla Verde.* ☎ *787/268-2329.*

La Casa del Mar. This outfitter's boats are equipped for ocean dives; a two-tank dive is $150, including equipment. A PADI snorkel program, at $65 per person, is also available. *El Conquistador Resort & Country Club, Fajardo.* ☎ *787/863-1000.*

Sea Ventures Dive Center. Sea Ventures offers a $95 two-tank dive. It's just farther east along Hwy. 3 beyond the exit for El Conquistador. *Puerto del Rey Marina, Rte. 3 Km 51.4, Fajardo.* ☎ *787/863-3483.*

Taino Divers. This outfitter offers scuba and snorkel trips, as well as boat charters and fishing tours. A day trip to Desecheo Island Natural Reserve, just off Rincón's coast, leaves at 10am and returns at 2pm. Snorkeling runs $75, and a two-tank dive is $110. Half-day fishing charters are $725. Sunset sails and whale watching trips in the winter cost $35 per person. *Black Eagle Marina at Rincón. Rte. 413 final, Rincón.* ☎ *787/823-6429.*

Fishing for Marlin.

Humpback whale.

Dive Center. This PADI facility has two custom boats that hold up to 10 divers and offers snorkeling and scuba half-day trips for $75; a two-tank dive costs $135 to $185. Snorkeling trips, including lunch and drinks, are $95. The *Río Mar Beach Resort & Spa: A Wyndham Grand*

Scuba Diving.

Property, Río Mar Blvd. 6000, Río Grande. ☎ *787/888-6000.*

Sea Venture Dive Copamarina. Part of the Copamarina Beach Resort, this outfitter takes adventurers to beautiful spots in Puerto Rico's underexplored southwestern waters. A two-tank dive costs $119, with full diving equipment. Reserve in advance. *Copamarina Beach Resort. Rte. 333 Km 6.5, Caña Gorda, Guánica.* ☎ *787/821-0505, ext. 729.*

★ **Palmas Dive Center.** Its 44-foot-long (13m) dive boat makes jaunts to the dive sites surrounding the center of the east coast, near Monkey Island, home to an escaped colony of former lab animals. Scuba trips cost as little as $99; half-day snorkeling $60. *Palmas del Mar, Anchors Village, 110 Harbor Dr., Humacao.* ☎ *787/863-3483.*

Surfing/Windsurfing/ Kite-surfing

If you want to learn to surf, windsurf, or kite-board, or perfect your technique while in Puerto Rico, there's ample opportunity. Puerto

Rico's northwest surfing beaches are world famous, but its entire north coast is dotted with breaks, including San Juan, which has more than its fair share. The northwest from Isabela to Rincón has several famous spots, like Wilderness, Middles, Jobos, Crashboat, Las Marías, the Spanish Wall, and Las Palmas. In San Juan, surfing beaches include La 8, just outside of Old San Juan in Puerta de Tierra, near Escambrón Beach, and Pine Grove in Isla Verde, a great spot to learn because of its small, steady, well-formed waves. Windsurfing and kite-boarding are also increasingly popular, with Ocean Park and Punta Las Marias the best places to go in the San Juan metropolitan area. Other spots on the island for windsurfing include Santa Isabel, Guánica, and La Parguera in the south; Jobos and Shacks in the northwest; and the Island of Culebra off the east coast.

Walking on Water Surfing School.

Professional surfer William Sue-A-Quan and a small crew of instructors will get you standing up on your first day, showing you how fun the sport of surfing can be. He's a great teacher and takes on students as young as 5 and as old as 75. Although it's based on Pine Grove Beach, Sue-A-Quan runs surf tours throughout the island. Lessons start at $60 per hour. ☎ 787/955-6059. www.gosurfpr.com.

Aquatica Dive, Bike and Surf Adventures.

This full-service dive and surf shop also rents equipment and gives lessons in scuba and surfing. The outfit also runs mountain-bike excursions to the Guajataca Forest. Prices depend on season and group size, but surf lessons cost $45 to $65 for 90 minutes and a two-tank scuba dive is $60 to $85. Bicycle tours cost between $45 and $65 and last up to 3 hours. Surf and scuba equipment rentals run from $20 to $45 per day, while bicycles are $25 per day. *Rte. 110 Km 10, outside gate 5, Rafael Hernández Airport, Aguadilla.* ☎ 787/890-6071.

Hang Loose Surf Shop.

This well-stocked shop gives surf lessons ($55-per-hour private lessons) and

Windsurfing.

Kite-surfing.

rents boards for $25 daily. The shop is owned by Werner Vega, a great big wave rider, who is one of Puerto Rico's premier board shapers. *Rte. 4466 Km 1.2, Playa Jobos, Isabela.* ☎ *787/872-2490. Tues–Sun 10am–5pm.*

Puntas Surf School. This surf school is run by expatriate surfing enthusiasts Melissa Taylor and Bill Woodward. Lessons start at around $50 per hour. *P.O. Box 4319, HC-01, Calle Vista del Mar.* ☎ *787/823-3618 or 207/251-1154. www.puntassurf school.com.*

Rincón Surf School. This comprehensive school offers beginner, intermediate, and advanced lessons and 1-day, 3-day, and week-long packages. *P.O. Box 1333, Rincón.* ☎ *787/823-0610. www.rinconsurf school.com.*

Velauno. This well-stocked surf shop specializes in windsurfing and kite-surfing lessons, rentals, and sales. Beginner's classes with equipment rental in either kite- or windsurfing are $150; private lessons with gear included are $50 an hour. One-day rental costs for windsurfing gear are $75; 3 days $150; and 1 week $225. For kite-surfing gear, it's $40 1-day; $90 3 days; and $130 for the week. *Calle Loíza 2430, Punta Las Marías, San Juan.* ☎ *787/982-0543 or 787/728-8716. www. velauno.com.* ●

The
Savvy Traveler

Before You Go

Government Tourist Offices

For information before you leave home, visit www.gotopuertorico.com. There are several tourism-related websites on Puerto Rico. The best, with the most accurate and current information, tend to be homegrown sites catering to local businesses in specific destinations like Rincón or Vieques. These include The Tourism Association of Rincón (www.rincon.org), Insider's Guide to South Puerto Rico (www.letsgotoponce.com), the Vieques website Enchanted Isles (www.enchanted-isle.com), Discover Culebra (www.culebra-island.com), and Puerto Rico Travel Maps (www.travelmaps.com). In Puerto Rico, you can visit or contact the Puerto Rico Tourism Company main Old San Juan office at La Princesa Building, Paseo La Princesa 2 (☎ 800/866-7827 or 787/721-2400). There are also offices at Luis Muñoz Marin Airport (☎ 787/791-1014) daily from 9am to 10pm. Another office is at La Casita, Pier 1, Old San Juan (☎ 787/722-1709), open Saturday to Wednesday 9am to 8pm, Thursday and Friday 8:30am to 6:30pm.

The Best Times to Go

Besides perhaps late August and September (the absolute height of hurricane season and wettest time of the year) there is not a bad time to come to Puerto Rico. Most visitors come in the winter to escape cold temperatures and snow elsewhere, and that's certainly a fine time to come. Visitors, however, will feel summer surprisingly agreeable too. Puerto Rico's climate varies little, with year-round temperatures ranging from 75° to 85°F (24°–29°C). San Juan and the northern coast tend to

be cooler and wetter than Ponce and the southern coast. The coolest weather is in the central mountains. Though temperatures can soar, the trade winds usually ensure comfortable days and nights.

Festivals & Special Events

Just about every weekend, there are Fiestas Patronales, or Patron Saint Festivals, thrown to honor town saints. They offer some of the top acts in island music for free, activities for children, great food, and drinks at reasonable prices. Other top festivals are listed below.

WINTER. Las Navidades (the Christmas Season). Throughout the season, Old San Juan has spiffy displays, artisan fairs, and Christmas decor in its plazas. A Christmas fair is set up on the outskirts of San Cristóbal Fort in Plaza San Juan Bautista in front of the Capitol in Puerta de Tierra just outside Old San Juan. From after Thanksgiving through Three Kings Day on January 6.

The **Bacardi Artisans' Fair** features more than 100 artisans who turn out to exhibit and sell their wares. The fair includes shows for adults and children, a Puerto Rican troubadour contest, rides, and typical food and drink—all sold by nonprofit organizations. It is held on the grounds of the world's largest rum-manufacturing plant in Cataño, right across San Juan Bay from the Old City. For more information, call ☎ 787/788-1500. www.bacardi.com. First 2 Sundays in December.

Hatillo Masks Festival, Hatillo. Held on the Day of the Innocents, this is one of the island's best traditional festivals. The day stems from the biblical story of King Herod

Previous page: Old San Juan.

PUERTO RICO'S AVERAGE MONTHLY TEMPERATURES

	JAN	FEB	MAR	APR	MAY	JUNE
TEMP. (°F)	75	75	76	78	79	81
TEMP. (°C)	25	24	24	24.4	25.6	26

	JULY	AUG	SEPT	OCT	NOV	DEC
TEMP. (°F)	81	81	81	81	79	77
TEMP. (°C)	27	27	27	27	27	26

ordering the death of all infant boys in an attempt to kill the baby Jesus, but today in Puerto Rico it is a time to tell tall tales, much like April Fool's Day. Men with colorful masks and costumes chase each other through town on horseback, and there are elaborately created floats during a procession. Of course, there's also food, music, and crafts exhibits. For more information, call ☎ 787/898-4040. December 28.

Three Kings Day. This is the day, more so than even Christmas, that children here look forward to receiving gifts. There are a number of festivals across the island, but the biggest takes place in Juana Díaz, outside Ponce on the southwest coast, with a breathtaking recreation of the Three Kings of the Orient's journey to Bethlehem; the procession begins at a museum built to commemorate the annual event and leads to the town square, where there is a beautiful mass, with biblical scenes recreated by actors. Information in Spanish about the festival is available at www.reyesdejuanadiaz.com or call the Three Kings Council (☎ 787/260-0817). January 6.

San Sebastián Street Festival. For many San Juan residents, Christmas is not over until the Fiestas de la Calle San Sebastián. Held along Calle San Sebastián in Old San Juan, this big street party is an artisan fair by day and a raucous rumba at night. It takes place during a long weekend, Thursday through Sunday, in mid-January. For more information, call ☎ 787/721-2400. Mid-January.

The **San Blas Half-Marathon** in Coamo, on the south coast, draws international and local runners who compete in a challenging 13-mile (21km) half-marathon in the hilly south-central town of Coamo. Call Delta Phi Delta Fraternity (☎ 787/825-2775; www.maratonsanblas.com). Early February.

Coffee Harvest Festival. Folk music, a parade of floats, typical foods, crafts, and demonstrations of coffee preparation are hallmarks of Maricao's famous festival. For more information, call ☎ 787/838-2290 or 787/267-5536. Second week of February.

Carnival Ponceño. Ponce is the place to be on Fat Tuesday, with costumed revelers, parades, floats, dancing, and street parties. The city is known for the bright, horned masked worn by revelers. For more information, call ☎ 787/284-4141. Mid-February.

Casals Festival. Held mostly at the Luis A. Ferré Performing Arts Center in San Juan, this is one of the Caribbean's most noted cultural events. Begun by renowned cellist Pablo Casals, it has been attracting top talent in the classical music world since 1957, the same year he also founded the Puerto Rico Symphony Orchestra. Tickets range from $30 to $40, but a 50% discount is offered to students, people over 60, and persons with disabilities. Tickets are available through the Puerto Rico Symphonic Orchestra in San Juan (☎ 787/721-7727), the Luis A. Ferré Performing Arts Center (☎ 787/620-4444), or Ticket Center (☎ 787/792-5000). Information is also available from the Casals Festival (☎ 787/721-8370; www.festcasalspr.gobierno.pr). Late February to early March.

SPRING. Holy Week leading up to Easter is a big vacation week, when virtually the entire island shuts down. Coastal resorts jam with local vacationers, but San Juan hosts a bunch of activities. On Good Friday in Old San Juan, an artful and moving procession of the cross with costumed actors leads to the steps of the San Juan Cathedral. Good Friday.

San Germán's **Sugar Harvest Festival** has live music, crafts, and typical foods. Late April.

Heineken JazzFest (www.pr heinekenjazz.com) has become one of the premier Latin jazz festivals in the world. It is currently held in the Tito Puente Amphitheatre set against Hato Rey's Parque Luis Muñoz Marín, a gorgeous setting. Tickets are available through www.ticketpop.com or ☎ 787/294-0001. Late May and early June.

SUMMER. Summer really gets underway with the **San Juan Bautista Fiesta,** when islanders go to the beach at night and at midnight, walk backward into the sea three times for good luck in the coming year. Throughout San Juan, the beaches are packed with revelers from late afternoon to midnight and hotels offer top entertainment. Beginning on the eve of the feast day of San Juan the Baptist on June 24.

The **Aibonito Flower Festival,** at Road 721 next to the City Hall Coliseum, in the central mountain town of Aibonito, has beautiful flowers, music, and good food. For more information, call ☎ 787/735-3871. Last week in June and first week in July.

One of the island's best patron saint festivals is the **Loíza Carnival** honoring St. John the Apostle. This town's African roots are on display with colorful processions, costumes, masks, and Afro-Caribbean music and dance. Call ☎ 787/876-1040. Late July through early August.

One of the region's premier game-fishing tournaments is the **International Billfish Tournament,** at San Juan's Club Náutico, San Juan. It draws international fishermen in pursuit of nearly 900-pound blue marlin and is one of the longest-running events of its kind. Call ☎ 787/722-0177. Late August or September.

FALL. Corozal has a **National Plantain Festival** in mid-October that is part arts and crafts show, musical performance, agricultural exhibition, and gastronomic fest. Call ☎ 787/859-3060. Mid-October. **Winter Baseball League** sees six Puerto Rican professional clubs compete; it attracts professionals from North America to play as well as top local players. November and December.

Jayuya hosts its **Indian Festival,** which features the culture and tradition of the Taíno Indians, including their music, food, and games. There are also arts, crafts, music, and food, plus a Miss Taíno Indian Pageant. Call ☎ 787/828-2020. Second week of November.

Puerto Rico Discovery Day commemorates the "discovery" by Columbus in 1493 of Puerto Rico, but today is celebrated as an affirmation of the African, Taíno, and European roots of Puerto Rico's culture. Late November.

Take Me Out to the *Beisbol* Game

Baseball has a long, illustrious history in Puerto Rico. Imported around the turn of the 20th century by plantation owners as a leisure activity for workers, *beisbol* quickly caught fire, and local leagues have produced such major-league stars as Roberto Alomar, Bernie Williams, and the late great Roberto Clemente. Current stars include Carlos Delgado, Jorge Posada, Iván Rodríguez, Carlos Beltrán, and the Molina brothers. A top-notch league of six teams—featuring many rising professionals honing their skills during the winter months—holds its season November through January and plays in ballparks throughout Puerto Rico. This is a chance to see good baseball in a more intimate setting than is afforded in the U.S. major leagues.

Getting **There**

By Plane

As the major airline hub of the Caribbean Basin, Puerto Rico is by far the most accessible of the Caribbean islands. See "Toll-Free Numbers and Websites" on p 177 for airlines serving Puerto Rico.

Getting **Around**

By Plane

Cape Air flies from Luis Muñoz Marín International Airport to Mayagüez, Ponce, and Vieques several times a day. They also offer many flights daily to St. Thomas, St. Croix, and Tortola. See p 177.

By Car

Puerto Rico offers some of the most scenic drives in all the Caribbean. Driving around and discovering its little hidden beaches, coastal towns, mountain villages, vast forests, and national parks is reason enough to visit. You'll need a car to explore it well. Local drivers can be maddening, though, as can the legendary traffic jams around cities. Beware that some roads, especially in the mountainous interior, are too narrow or poorly maintained for comfort. Avis, Budget, and Hertz are on the island, and reputable local outfits include Charlie Car Rental and Target Car Rental. Distances are often posted in kilometers rather than miles (1km = 0.62 mile), but speed limits are displayed in miles per hour. See p 177.

GASOLINE In Puerto Rico, gasoline is sold by the liter, not by the gallon. The cost of gasoline is comparable to prices in the continental United States.

DRIVING RULES Speed limits are given in miles per hour. Most highways are either 55 mph or a combination of 55 mph and 65 mph.

BREAKDOWNS & ASSISTANCE

Make arrangements ahead of time with your rental agency about what to do in case of an accident or breakdown and ask for backup emergency services and numbers. The **American Automobile Association (AAA)** has a Puerto Rico Chapter (654 Muñoz Rivera Ave., Lobby Level, Ste. 103–1119, Hato Rey; ☎ 787/620-7805).

By Bus

The **Metropolitan Bus Authority** (☎ 787/767-7979) operates buses in the greater San Juan area. Bus stops are marked by upright metal signs or yellow posts that say PARADA. The bus terminal is the dock area in the same building as the Covadanga parking lot next to the Treasury Department. Fares are 75¢.

This section of Old San Juan is the starting point for many of the city's metropolitan bus routes. One useful route is the A5, which hits downtown Santurce, Avenida de Diego near Condado, then goes along Loíza Street and down Isla Verde's oceanfront drive where all the hotels are located. You can switch to the B21 at De Diego Street if you want to go down Condado's main drive, Avenida Ashford.

The B21 runs from Old San Juan to Condado, while also servicing Plaza Las Américas.

The privately run MetroBus runs express buses between Old San Juan and Río Piedras, with stops in Hato Rey and Santurce.

Any bus marked ATI hooks up with the Tren Urbano, probably at its Sagrado Corazón Station, which is its last stop into the city. The ticket costs $1.50 but includes a transfer to the train.

By Train

Tren Urbano (☎ 866/900-1284; www.ati.gobierno.pr) links San Juan to suburbs like Santurce, Bayamón, and Guaynabo. During rush hour (5–9am and 3–6pm), the train operates every 8 minutes; otherwise, it runs every 12 minutes. There is no service daily from 11:20pm to 5:30am. The fare is $1.50 one-way and includes a transfer to buses. It's a beautiful ride and gives tourists a different experience of the city; the train passes on an elevated track through the modern Hato Rey financial district, plunges underground in Río Piedras, then snakes through upscale suburban neighborhoods, with tropical foliage and pools visible in many backyards. The fare includes a transfer because a special class of buses has been created to link up with particular Tren Urbano routes.

By Public Cars

Cars and minibuses known as públicos provide low-cost transportation around the island. Their license plates have the letters "P" or "PD" following the numbers. They serve all the main towns of Puerto Rico; passengers are let off and picked up along the way, both at designated stops and when someone flags them down. Rates are set by the Public Service Commission. Públicos usually operate during daylight hours, departing from the main plaza of a town. There are several operators listed under "Lineas de Carros" in the local Yellow Pages. It costs about $25 from San Juan to just about anywhere on the island. Serving San Juan and Mayagüez is **Lineas Sultana,** Calle Esteban González 898, Urbanización Santa Rita, Río Piedras (☎ 787/765-9377). San Juan–Ponce routes are handled by **Choferes Unidos de Ponce,** Terminal de Carros Públicos, Calle Vive, in Ponce (☎ 787/764-0540).

By Taxi

Taxi service is available throughout the island. In San Juan, there is a flat-rate system for major destinations. The island's **Puerto Rico Tourism**

Puerto Rico's Beautiful Beaches

Puerto Rico and its offshore islands and cays are surrounded by hundreds of miles of beachfront. There are silky white-sand beaches fronted by the warmest blue sea, windswept rocky coastlines splitting surging tides, and classic palm-fringed shores pummeled by Atlantic waves that are the stuff of surfer dreams. Many of the beaches are alternately fierce or calm, depending on the weather or the time of year, and many are fronted by aquamarine waters brimming with reefs and tropical fish.

Beaches, even those fronting resorts, are public property, so access is guaranteed to all by the Puerto Rico Constitution. Camping on beaches is illegal except in designated areas, but it is common practice in rural areas.

Company (Transportation Division; ☎ 787/999-2100 or 787/253-0418) establishes flat rates between well-traveled areas within San Juan. From Luis Muñoz Marín International Airport to Isla Verde, $10; to Condado, $15; and to Old San Juan, $19. There are also set fees from the cruise-ship piers outside of Old San Juan to set destinations: Isla Verde, $19; Condado, $12; and Old San Juan, $7. You will be charged 50¢ per bag for your first three bags and $1 per bag thereafter. Metered fares start off with an initial charge of $1.75, plus $1.90 per mile, and a 10¢ charge is applied for each 25 seconds of waiting time. Tolls are not included in either fare. Normal tipping supplements of between 10% and 15% of these fares are appreciated.

Although meters are supposed to be used, on most trips outside the zoned rates, drivers will probably offer you a flat rate of their own devising. San Juan cabbies are loath to use the meter. Taxis are invariably lined up outside the entrance to most of the island's hotels, and if they're not, a staff member can almost always call one for you. If you need to arrange a taxi on your own, some reliable operators in San Juan are **Metro Taxis** (☎ 787/725-2870), the **Rochdale Cab Company** (☎ 787/721-1900), or the **Major Cab Company** (☎ 787/723-2460).

Fast **Facts**

ATMS ATMs are linked to a network that most likely includes your bank at home. **Cirrus** (☎ 800/424-7787; www.mastercard.com) and **Plus** (☎ 800/843-7587; www.visa.com) are the two most popular networks in the U.S. Puerto Rico has a very developed network and nearly all merchants accept payments with a bank card.

BABYSITTING The best place to check is with your hotel. Many hotels have babysitting services or will provide you with lists of reliable sitters. The better services also include organized activities for children.

BANKING HOURS Bank hours are generally Monday through Friday from 8:30am to 4pm, but many banks offer extended hours at some branches. Generally, extended hours last until 7pm during the week, plus banking Saturdays and Sundays between 9am and noon.

B&BS The Puerto Rico Tourism Company flags a number of inns and guesthouses under the *paradores puertorriqueños.* They are spread throughout the island, from the interior to the coasts. Most have pools, and all offer excellent Puerto Rican cuisine. Many are within easy driving distance of San Juan.

Properties must meet certain benchmark standards of quality to be admitted to the program so that tourists feel comfortable staying at the property. One complaint about the program is that variances in quality still range widely from one property to the next. For more information, call ☎ 800/866-7827 or go to www.gotoparadores.com.

The Tourism Company also operates a similar program that promotes local restaurants, called **Mesones Gastronómicos** (☎ 800/ 981-7575). Restaurants in this program also have to pass muster with the Tourism Company for inclusion.

BUSINESS HOURS Regular business hours are Monday through Friday from 8am to 5pm. Shopping hours vary considerably. Regular shopping hours are Monday through Thursday and Saturday from 9am to 6pm. On Friday, stores have a long day: 9am to 9pm. Many stores also open on Sunday from 11am to 5pm.

CLIMATE Puerto Rico has a steady year-round climate with average temperatures only varying from 75° to 85°F (24°–29°C). The island is wettest and hottest in August, averaging 81°F (27°C) with 7 inches (18cm) of rain. Hurricane season lasts from June 1 to November 30, but the most damaging storms have historically struck from late August through September.

CONCERTS See chapter 2.

CONDOMINIUM, APARTMENT & VACATION HOME RENTALS One of the best ways to experience Old San Juan living is to rent a high-end furnished apartment. Keep in mind that getting a condo by the beach could save you a bundle over staying at a neighboring beachfront hotel, but you will give up little in terms of hotel amenities. Many Old City rentals are historic with high ceilings, open balconies, beautiful rooftop terraces, and verdant courtyards. Many rentals cater to discriminating travelers, offering first-rate creature comforts like Swedish mattresses and plush bathrobes, as well as upscale kitchens and bathrooms. Prices range from $500 weekly for a basic studio to $2,500 weekly for a three-bedroom, restored colonial beauty with rooftop terrace and ocean views. You'll pay a 7% tax and a cleaning fee of $75.The expert in Old City short-term rentals is **Vida Urbana** (Calle Cruz 255, Old San Juan, PR 00901; ☎ 787/587-3031; www.vidaurbanapr.com). Also try **Bóveda** (Calle Cristo 209, Old San Juan; ☎ 787/725-0263; www.boveda.info) and **The Caleta Guesthouse** (Caleta de las Monjas 11, Old San Juan; ☎ 787/725-5347). **Condado** and **Isla Verde** have an ample supply of furnished beachfront condos for short-term rentals, with weekly rates ranging from $525 to $2,250. In addition to their prime location, many of the condos have first-class pools and other facilities like tennis courts, health clubs, and beautiful common areas for picnics or gatherings. And they are within walking distance of the large hotels and area restaurants, clubs, and stores. Try **San Juan Vacations** (Cond. Marbella del Caribe, Ste. S-5, Isla Verde; ☎ 800/266-3639 or 787/727-1591; www.sanjuanvacations.com) or **Ronnie's Properties** (Calle Marseilles 14, Ritz Condominium, Ste. 11-F, San Juan; ☎ 787/722-1352; www.ronniesproperties.com).

CONSULATES & EMBASSIES Because Puerto Rico is part of the United States, there is no U.S. embassy. Several foreign governments have honorary consulates on the island, which often seek to foster commercial exchange and also offer their citizens assistance.

Canada. Av. Ponce de León 268, Ste. 802, San Juan, Hato Rey; ☎ 787/759-6629 or 787/294-1205.

United Kingdom. Urb. Palmanova, Calle Monaco 213, Humacao; ☎ 787/406-8777 or 787/285-2851.

CREDIT CARDS Credit cards are a safe way to "carry" money, they provide a convenient record of all your expenses, and they generally offer good exchange rates. You can also withdraw cash advances from your credit cards at banks or ATMs, provided you know your PIN.

CUSTOMS U.S. citizens do not need to clear Puerto Rican Customs upon arrival by plane or ship from the U.S. mainland. All non–U.S. citizens must clear Customs and are permitted to bring in items intended for their personal use, including tobacco, cameras, film, and a limited supply of liquor (usually 40 oz.). On departure, U.S.–bound travelers must have their luggage inspected by the U.S. Agriculture Department because laws prohibit bringing fruits and plants to the U.S. mainland. Fruits and vegetables are not allowed; but otherwise, you can bring back as many purchased goods as you want without

paying duty. Download the invaluable free pamphlet *Know Before You Go* online at www.cbp.gov. (Click on "Travel," and then click on "Know Before You Go! Online Brochure.") for more specifics.

DENTISTS If you have dental problems, a nationwide referral service known as **1-800-DENTIST** (☎ 800/336-8478) will provide the name of a nearby dentist or clinic. Several reputable dentists have offices in the Ashford Medical Center (Av. Ashford 1451; ☎ 787/721-6585) adjacent to the Ashford Presbyterian Community Hospital in Condado. Alternatively, look in the Yellow Pages under *dentistas*.

DINING Although there are many quality restaurants that allow casual dining attire, several of the finer restaurants in San Juan have upscale dress standards. Looking good is something of a national sport in Puerto Rico, so be prepared to get decked out, especially for a fancy meal.

DOCTORS See "Medical/Healthcare," below.

ELECTRICITY The United States uses 110 to 120 volts AC (60 cycles), compared to 220 to 240 volts AC (50 cycles) in most of Europe, Australia, and New Zealand. If your small appliances use 220 to 240 volts, you'll need a 110-volt transformer and a plug adapter with two flat parallel pins to operate them. Downward converters that change 220–240 volts to 110–120 volts are difficult to find in the United States, so bring one with you.

EMERGENCIES In an emergency, dial ☎ **911.** You can follow up with calls to **local police** (☎ 787/726-7020), **fire department** (☎ 787/725-3444), or medical emergency line (☎ 787/754-2550). For the **Poison Control Center,** call ☎ 800/362-3585.

FAMILY TRAVEL   Puerto Ricans love kids and take them everywhere, so don't be shy in bringing your little ones anywhere, from finer restaurants to musical performances. There is also so much to do with the family because of the island's tourism attractions, including watersports and other adventures.

GAY & LESBIAN TRAVELERS   Several national gay websites offer ample travel information on Puerto Rico, including the **International Gay & Lesbian Travel Association (IGLTA;** ☎ 800/448-8550 or 954/776-2626; www.iglta.org), which has an online directory of gay- and lesbian-friendly lodgings, bars, and other businesses. A good local tourist site for gay and lesbian visitors is produced by www.orgulloboricua.net. Access the informative English-language section directly at www.orgulloboricua.net/touristbrief/gayscene.html.

HOLIDAYS   Puerto Rico has many public holidays when stores, offices, and schools are closed: New Year's Day, Three Kings Day (Jan 6), Presidents' Day (late Feb), Good Friday (Mar or Apr), Memorial Day (last Mon in May), July 4th, Labor Day (first Mon in Sept), Thanksgiving (third Thurs in Nov), Veterans Day (Nov 11), and Christmas (Dec 25), plus such local holidays as Constitution Day (July 25) and Discovery Day (Nov 19). Remember, U.S. federal holidays are holidays in Puerto Rico, too.

INSURANCE   Trip-cancellation insurance helps you get your money back if you have to back out of a trip, if you have to go home early, or if your travel supplier goes bankrupt. Allowed reasons for cancellation can range from sickness to natural disasters to the State Department declaring your destination unsafe for travel. In this unstable world, trip-cancellation

insurance is a good buy if you're getting tickets well in advance. Insurance policy details vary, so read the fine print—and especially make sure that your airline or cruise line is on the list of carriers covered in case of bankruptcy. For information, contact one of the following insurers: **Access America** (☎ 866/807-3982; www.accessamerica.com); **Travel Guard International** (☎ 800/826-4919; www.travelguard.com); **Travel Insured International** (☎ 800/243-3174; www.travelinsured.com); or **Travelex Insurance Services** (☎ 888/457-4602; www.travelex-insurance.com).

Although it's not required of travelers, health insurance is highly recommended. Unlike many European countries, the United States does not usually offer free or low-cost medical care to its citizens or visitors. Doctors and hospitals are expensive, and in most cases will require advance payment or proof of coverage before they render their services. Though lack of health insurance may prevent you from being admitted to a hospital in non-emergencies, don't worry about being left on a street corner to die: The American way is to fix you now and bill the living daylights out of you later.

INTERNET ACCESS   Major hotels and even small B&Bs have Internet access; many of them also have Wi-Fi in public areas and rooms (ask about charges ahead of time). Wi-Fi is also available in many public plazas, fast-food restaurants, and public buildings. **Cybernet Cafe** (Av. Ashford Condado 1128; ☎ 787/724-4033) is open Monday to Thursday from 9am to 11pm, Friday and Saturday from 9am to midnight, and Sunday from 10am to 10pm. It charges $3 for 20 minutes, $5 for 35 minutes, $7 for 50 minutes, and $9 for 65 minutes. A second location with the same hours and pricing is in Isla Verde at Av. Isla Verde 5980 (☎ 787/728-4195).

MAIL & POSTAGE   To find the nearest **post office,** call ☎ 800/ASK-USPS or log on to www.usps.gov. Because the U.S. Postal Service is responsible for handling mail on Puerto Rico, the regulations and tariffs are the same as on the mainland United States. Stamps can be purchased at any post office, all of which are open Monday through Friday from 8am to 5pm. Saturday hours are from 8am to noon (closed Sun). As on the mainland, you can purchase stamps at vending machines in airports, stores, and hotels.

MEDICAL/HEALTHCARE   The **Ashford Presbyterian Community Hospital** has emergency medical care, a children's emergency room, as well as an adjacent medical center filled with doctors' offices (Av. Ashford 1451; ☎ 787/721-6585; Condado). Service is also provided at **Clínica Las Américas,** Franklin Delano Roosevelt Ave. 400, Hato Rey (☎ 787/765-1919), and at **Puerto Rico Medical Center,** Av. Americo Miranda, Río Piedras (☎ 787/777-3535).

MONEY   There's no need to carry a lot of cash. U.S. currency is the official currency, and most establishments accept credit cards and most also accept payment directly from your bank card without any added fees. ATM machines are everywhere; the highest fee you will pay is $1.50. Traveler's checks are also unnecessary and something of an anachronism. The currency-exchange facilities at any large international bank within Puerto Rico's larger cities can exchange non-U.S. currencies for dollars. It's advisable to handle your exchange needs in

San Juan if you are heading to rural Puerto Rico.

PASSPORTS   Always keep a photocopy of your passport with you (but separate from your passport) when you're traveling. If your passport is lost or stolen, having a copy significantly facilitates the reissuing process at your consulate. Keep your passport and other valuables in your room's safe or in the hotel safe. American citizens traveling from the United States don't need a passport to visit Puerto Rico.

PHARMACIES   There are large Walgreens throughout Puerto Rico, including Old San Juan, Condado, Isla Verde, near Ocean Park, and in Miramar. One of the most centrally located pharmacies in Old San Juan is the **Puerto Rican Drug Co.** (Calle San Francisco 157; ☎ 787/725-2202), open daily from 7:30am to 9:30pm.

SAFETY   Crime exists in Puerto Rico, but a little common sense and basic precautions go a long way toward keeping you safe. Theft and muggings are rare in tourism districts, but confine your moonlit beach nights to the fenced-in and guarded areas around some of the major hotels. Avoid isolated streets, beaches, and rural areas at night.

SENIOR TRAVELERS   Discounts of as much as 50% for seniors are available at most attractions, movies, and theatrical performances. Seniors are also entitled to expedited service at government agencies.

TAXES   All hotel rooms in Puerto Rico are subject to a tax, which is not included in the rates given in this book. At casino hotels, the tax is 11%; at noncasino hotels, it's 9%. At country inns you pay a 7% tax. Most hotels also add a 10% service charge. If they don't, you're

Beware Dengue Fever

Although mosquitoes are a nuisance, they do not carry malaria in Puerto Rico. However, after a long absence, the dreaded dengue fever has returned to Puerto Rico. The disease is transmitted by the Aede mosquito, and its symptoms include fever, headaches, pain in the muscles and joints, skin blisters, and hemorrhaging. Most of its victims lack any defense against it. You should wear bug spray at all times, especially on beaches and on the islands of Vieques and Culebra.

expected to tip for services rendered. When you're booking a room, it's always best to inquire about these added charges. There is now a 7% sales tax on a broad range of goods and services. There is no airport departure tax.

TAXIS See p 59.

TELEPHONE For directory assistance, dial 411; for long-distance information, dial 1, then the appropriate area code and 555-1212. Pay phones cost 75¢ for local calls. Puerto Rico has two area codes (787) and (939), so all calls require dialing the full area code and number.

TIPPING Tipping expectations mirror those on the U.S. mainland: 15% in restaurants and bars, for taxis, and for other services.

A Brief **History**

100 A.D. Amerindian nomadic cave-dwellers establish themselves in Puerto Rico.

300 A.D. The Arawaks migrate to Puerto Rico from the Orinoco Basin in Venezuela.

1493 The Taínos develop from a subsequent Amerindian group and inhabit Puerto Rico when Columbus arrives during his second voyage in 1493, marking the start of 5 centuries of Spanish rule. Taíno words and place names are still used in modern-day Puerto Rico. New studies confirm Amerindian genes live on in today's islanders.

1508 Spanish conquistador Juan Ponce de León discovers gold, conquers the Taínos, and then becomes Puerto Rico's first governor.

1521 The island is named Puerto Rico (Rich Port) and takes on strategic importance for the Spanish Crown.

1540 Construction begins on La Fortaleza, which is still in use today as the Governor's Mansion.

1595 The English invade Puerto Rico, occupy it for 2 months, but then flee as islanders stage guerilla warfare and tropical disease hits the invaders hard.

1625 The Dutch attack El Morro and burn San Juan, but are beaten back by Spanish forces. In response, the city's huge fortifications are built. They still dominate Old San Juan.

1797 British fail to conquer Puerto Rico in a huge invasion.

1865 Representatives from Puerto Rico and other Spanish colonies like Cuba and the Philippines go to Madrid to air their grievances as part of a process of liberalizing Spanish colonial policy.

1868 The Grito de Lares takes place when a group of Puerto Ricans seize the town of Lares from the Spanish for the new republic of Puerto Rico, but the plotters are quickly smashed back by the Spanish military. Independence supporters today mark this anniversary.

1895 The revolution in Cuba increases demands for greater autonomy of Puerto Rico.

1898 The U.S. battleship *Maine* blows up in the harbor of Havana, killing 266 men and sparking the Spanish-American War.

1898 American troops land at Guánica, beginning a more than century-old relationship with the United States.

1898 The Treaty of Paris, which set the terms of Spain's surrender, makes Puerto Rico a territory of the United States.

1899 A hurricane destroys cities and kills 3,000.

1900 Puerto Rico is recognized as an unincorporated territory with its governor named by the president of the United States, who retains the exclusive right to override the island governor's veto.

1932 A devastating hurricane, on the heels of a previous one 4 years before, increases poverty and hunger and destroys crops and buildings.

1935 President Franklin D. Roosevelt starts the Puerto Rican Reconstruction Administration to develop agriculture, public works, and expanding electricity.

1937 A bloody incident, remembered as the Ponce Massacre, takes the lives of 17 citizens and two police officers after Puerto Rican Nationalist Party marchers and police cross paths.

1938 Luis Muñoz Marín, son of the statesman Luis Muñoz Rivera, founds the Popular Democratic Party under the slogan "Bread, Land, and Liberty."

1940 The PDP gains legislative majorities and Muñoz becomes the head of the Senate.

1946 President Harry S Truman appoints native-born Jesús Piñero as governor of Puerto Rico.

1948 Luis Muñoz Marín becomes the first elected governor of Puerto Rico.

1950 Pedro Albizu Campos and his Nationalist Party attempt an unsuccessful uprising, which includes a foiled plot to kill President Harry Truman.

1952 The Commonwealth of Puerto Rico is born when Puerto Ricans in a 3-to-1 vote ratify a local constitution, which is approved by Congress. It establishes the parameters of its relationship with the United States, which continues to be the law of the land today.

1954 A group of four Puerto Rican nationalists shoot up the House of Representatives from the visitors' gallery, wounding five representatives, one seriously. The attackers include Lolita Lebrón, who shouts "I did not come to kill but to die for Puerto Rico!"

1967 Puerto Ricans overwhelmingly choose to maintain the current commonwealth status in the first political plebiscite held since the enactment of commonwealth. The status wins a subsequent referendum in 1993, while the final vote in 1999 only muddies waters further with a "none of the above" option winning.

1968 Luis A. Ferré is elected governor for the pro-statehood Partido Nuevo Progresista, or New Progressive Party, which begins a strong two-majority party system that continues to the present.

1979 Puerto Rico hosts the Pan-American Games.

1996 Puerto Rico sees the start of a 10-year phase-out of its federal industrial incentives, Section 936 and Section 30A, marking the end of a 50-year-old industrial-development program on the island supported by federal tax credits.

1999 A Navy bombing run kills a local resident on its Vieques training ground, exposing decades of pent-up anger over military indifference and abuses.

2003 Widespread protests over another deadly bombing force the military to abandon Vieques, a move that prompts its decision to close its massive military base in Ceiba, Naval Station Roosevelt Roads.

Useful **Terms & Phrases**

Most Puerto Ricans are very patient with those who try to speak their language; it helps a lot to know a few basic phrases. Included here are simple phrases for expressing basic needs, followed by some common menu items.

ENGLISH	SPANISH	PRONUNCIATION
Good day	**Buen día**	Bwehn *dee*-ah
Good morning	**Buenos días**	*Bweh*-nohs dee-ahs
How are you?	**¿Cómo está?**	*Koh*-moh eh-*stah*
Very well	**Muy bien**	Mwee byehn
Thank you	**Gracias**	*Grah*-syahs
You're welcome	**De nada**	Deh *nah*-dah
Goodbye	**Adiós**	Ah-*dyohs*
Please	**Por favor**	Pohr fah-*bohr*
Yes	**Sí**	See
No	**No**	Noh
Excuse me	**Perdóneme**	Pehr-*doh*-neh-meh
Give me	**Déme**	*Deh*-meh
Where is . . . ?	**¿Dónde está . . . ?**	*Dohn*-deh eh-*stah*
the station	**la estación**	lah eh-stah-*syohn*
a hotel	**un hotel**	oon oh-*tehl*
a gas station	**una gasolinera**	oo-nah gah-soh-lee-neh-rah
a restaurant	**un restaurante**	oon res-tow-rahn-teh

ENGLISH	SPANISH	PRONUNCIATION
the toilet	**el baño**	el *bah*-nyoh
a good doctor	**un buen médico**	oon bwehn *meh*-dee-coh
the road to . . .	**el camino a/hacia**	el cah-*mee*-noh ah/ah-syah
To the right	**A la derecha**	Ah lah deh-*reh*-chah
To the left	**A la izquierda**	Ah lah ees-*kyehr*-dah
Straight ahead	**Derecho**	Deh-*reh*-choh
I would like	**Quisiera**	Key-*syeh*-rah
I want	**Quiero**	Kyeh-roh
to eat	**comer**	koh-*mehr*
a room	**una habitación**	*oo*-nah ah-bee-tah-*syohn*
Do you have . . . ?	**¿Tiene usted . . . ?**	Tyeh-neh oo-*sted*
a book	**un libro**	oon *lee*-broh
a dictionary	**un diccionario**	oon deek-syoh-*nah*-ryoh
How much is it?	**¿Cuánto cuesta?**	*Kwahn*-toh kweh-stah
When?	**¿Cuándo?**	*Kwahn*-doh
What?	**¿Qué?**	Keh
There is (Is there . . . ?)	**(¿)Hay (. . . ?)**	Eye
What is there?	**¿Qué hay?**	Keh eye
Yesterday	**Ayer**	Ah-*yer*
Today	**Hoy**	Oy
Tomorrow	**Mañana**	Mah-*nyah*-nah
Good	**Bueno**	*Bweh*-noh
Bad	**Malo**	*Mah*-loh
Better (best)	**(Lo) Mejor**	(Loh) Meh-*hohr*
More	**Más**	Mahs
Less	**Menos**	*Meh*-nohs
No smoking	**Se prohibe fumar**	Seh proh-*ee*-beh foo-*mahr*
Postcard	**Tarjeta postal**	Tar-*heh*-tah poh-*stahl*
Insect repellent	**Repelente contra insectos**	Reh-peh-*lehn*-teh *cohn*-trah een-*sehk*-tohs

More Useful Phrases

ENGLISH	SPANISH	PRONUNCIATION
Do you speak English?	**¿Habla usted inglés?**	*Ah*-blah oo-*sted* een-*glehs*
Is there anyone here who speaks English?	**¿Hay alguien aqui que hable inglés?**	Eye *ahl*-gyehn ah-*kee* keh ah-bleh een-*glehs*
I speak a little Spanish.	**Hablo un poco de español.**	*Ah*-bloh oon *poh*-koh deh eh-spah-*nyohl*
I don't understand Spanish very well.	**No (lo) entiendo muy bien el español.**	Noh (loh) ehn-*tyehn*-doh mwee byehn el eh-spah-*nyohl*

ENGLISH	SPANISH	PRONUNCIATION
The meal is good.	Me gusta la comida.	Meh *goo*-stah lah koh-*mee*-dah
What time is it?	¿Qué hora es?	Keh *oh*-rah ehs
May I see your menu?	¿Puedo ver el menú?	*Pweh*-doh vehr el meh-*noo* (lah *car*-tah)
The check, please.	La cuenta, por favor.	Lah *kwehn*-tah pohr fa-*borh*
What do I owe you?	¿Cuánto le debo?	*Kwahn*-toh leh *deh*-boh
What did you say?	¿Cómo? (informal)	*Koh*-moh
I want (to see) . . .	Quiero (ver) . . .	*kyeh*-roh (vehr)
a room	un cuarto or una habitación	oon *kwar*-toh, *oo*-nah ah-bee-tah-*syohn*
for two	para dos	*pah*-rah dohs
persons	personas	pehr-*soh*-nahs
with (without) bathroom	con (sin) baño	kohn (seen) *bah*-nyoh
We are staying here only . . .	Nos quedamos aquí solamente . . .	Nohs keh-*dah*-mohs ah-*kee* soh-lah-*mehn*-teh
one night.	una noche.	*oo*-nah *noh*-cheh
one week.	una semana.	*oo*-nah seh-*mah*-nah
We are leaving . . .	Salimos . . .	Sah-*lee*-mohs
tomorrow.	mañana.	mah-*nya*-nah
Do you accept . . . ?	¿Acepta usted . . . ?	Ah-*sehp*-tah oo-*sted*
traveler's checks?	cheques de viajero?	*cheh*-kehs deh byah-*heh*-roh
Is there a laundromat . . . ? near here?	¿Hay una lavandería . . . ? cerca de aquí?	Eye *oo*-nah lah-*bahn*-deh-*ree*-ah *sehr*-kah deh ah-*kee*
Please send these clothes to the laundry.	Hágame el favor de mandar esta ropa a la lavandería.	*Ah*-gah-meh el fah-*borh* deh mahn-*dahr* eh-stah *roh*-pah a lah lah-*bahn*-deh-*ree*-ah

NUMBERS

ENGLISH	SPANISH	PRONUNCIATION
1	uno	oo-noh
2	dos	dohs
3	tres	trehs
4	cuatro	kwah-troh
5	cinco	seen-koh
6	seis	sayes
7	siete	syeh-teh
8	ocho	oh-choh
9	nueve	nweh-beh
10	diez	dyehs
11	once	ohn-seh
12	doce	doh-seh

ENGLISH	SPANISH	PRONUNCIATION
13	trece	treh-seh
14	catorce	kah-tohr-seh
15	quince	keen-seh
16	dieciséis	dyeh-see-sayes
17	diecisiete	dyeh-see-syeh-teh
18	dieciocho	dyeh-syoh-choh
19	diecinueve	dyeh-see-nweh-beh
20	veinte	bayn-teh
30	treinta	trayn-tah
40	cuarenta	kwah-ren-tah
50	cincuenta	seen-kwen-tah
60	sesenta	seh-sehn-tah
70	setenta	seh-tehn-tah
80	ochenta	oh-chehn-tah
90	noventa	noh-behn-tah
100	cien	syehn
200	doscientos	do-syehn-tohs
500	quinientos	kee-nyehn-tohs
1,000	mil	meel

Dining Terminology

Meals
desayuno   Breakfast.
almuerzo   Lunch.
cena   Supper.

Courses
tapa   A small serving of food that accompanies a beer or drink, usually served free of charge.
aperitivo   Appetizer.
sopa   Soup course. (Not necessarily a soup—it can be a dish of rice or noodles, called sopa seca [dry soup].)
ensalada   Salad.
entree   Main course.
postre   Dessert.

Miscellaneous Restaurant Terminology
cucharra   Spoon.
cuchillo   Knife.
la cuenta   The bill.
plato   Plate.
plato hondo   Bowl.
propina   Tip.
servilleta   Napkin.
tenedor   Fork.
vaso   Glass.
fonda   Strictly speaking, a food stall in the market or street, but now used in a loose or nostalgic sense to designate an informal restaurant.

Puerto Rican **Menu & Food Items**

achiote   Small red seed of the annatto tree, with mild flavor, used for both taste and color.
agua de coco   Chilled coconut juice, usually served right from the shell.

alcapurrias Fried plantain fritters stuffed with seafood, chicken, or meat.

asopao Hearty local rice stew with chicken, beans, shrimp, or other seafood.

adobo Dry-rub mixture of local sweet-and-mild spices.

amarillos Fried sweet plantains.

arroz Rice.

bacalaíto Codfish fritter.

bistec Steak.

buñuelos Fried pastry dusted with sugar. Can also mean a large, thin, crisp pancake that is dipped in boiling cane syrup.

café con leche Rich local coffee with steamed milk.

calabaza Zucchini squash.

caldo de pollo Chicken soup.

camarones Shrimp.

carne Meat.

cebolla Onion.

ceviche Fresh raw seafood marinated in oil and vinegar, onions, bay leaf, and mild spices.

chayote A type of spiny squash boiled and served as an accompaniment to meat dishes.

chillo Red snapper.

chimichurri Argentine sauce made with olive oil, oregano, parsley, and garlic, served with grilled meats.

Cubano Roast pork, ham, and Swiss cheese sandwich with pickles and mustard.

churrasco Latin skirt steak usually served grilled with a side of chimichurri sauce.

empanadilla A turnover with meat, chicken, seafood, and pizza stuffing.

fideo Noodle.

flan Custard.

gandules Pigeon peas served with rice or stew.

habichuelas Beans, usually pink beans.

huevos revueltos Scrambled eggs, often served with chopped ham.

huevos fritos Fried eggs, served with toast and ham.

lechón Roast pig.

lechuga Lettuce.

limón A small lime.

milanesa Beef cutlet breaded and fried.

mofongo Mashed plantain casserole.

mojo sauce Green sweet dipping sauce for fritters or fish.

morcilla Blood sausage.

pan de aqua Local bread, similar to French but infinitely airier.

papas Potatoes.

parrillada A sampler platter of grilled meats or seafood.

pastel A Puerto Rican tamale. A meat-filled plantain mash wrapped in green banana leaves.

pescado Fish. Common ways of cooking fish include al ajillo (sautéed with garlic), a la criolla (with sweet tomato and pepper sauce), a la plancha (grilled), frito (fried), and al horno (baked).

picadillo Any of several recipes using shredded beef, pork, or chicken.

platano Plantain.

pollo   Chicken. See pescado for common preparations.
pernil   Roast pork.
queso   Cheese.
ricao   Sweet green local herb, similar to cilantro.
res   Beef.
sofrito   A mixture of onion, garlic, sweet peppers, and recao that is used as a base from everything from soups to sautéed chicken.
tomate   Tomato.
tortilla   Spanish-style omelet.
tostones   Fried plantain discs.
viandas   Any number of local tuber vegetables served fried or boiled in a ceviche sauce, including platanos (plantains), batata (sweet potato), and yucca (cassava).

Toll-Free Numbers & Websites

Airlines on Puerto Rico

AIR CANADA
☎ 800/426-7000
www.aircanada.com

AMERICAN AIRLINES
☎ 800/433-7300
www.aa.com

BRITISH AIRWAYS
☎ 800/247-9297
www.ba.com

CAPE AIR
☎ 800/352-0714 or
/877/253-1121
www.flycapeair.com

CONTINENTAL AIRLINES
☎ 800/525-0280 or
787/890-2990
www.continental.com

DELTA
☎ 800/221-1212
www.delta.com

IBERIA
☎ 800/772-4642
www.iberia.com

JETBLUE
☎ 800/538-2583
www.jetblue.com

LUFTHANSA
☎ 800/399-LUFT
www.luftansa-usa.com

NORTHWEST/KLM
☎ 800/225-2525
www.nwa.com

SEABORNE AIRLINES
☎ 888/FLY-TOUR
www.flyseaborne.com

SPIRIT AIR
☎ 800/772-7117 or
787/772-7117
www.spiritair.com

UNITED AIRLINES
☎ 800/241-6522
www.united.com

US AIRWAYS
☎ 800/428-4322
www.usairways.com

Car-Rental Agencies on Puerto Rico

ALAMO
☎ 800/327-9633
www.goalamo.com

AVIS
☎ 800/321-3712
www.avis.com

BUDGET
☎ 800/572-0700
www.budget.com

CHARLIE CAR RENTAL
☎ 800/227-7368
www.charliecars.com

TARGET RENTAL CAR
☎ 787-782-6380
www.targetrentacar.com

DOLLAR
☎ 800/800-4000
www.dollarcar.com

HERTZ
☎ 800/654-3011
www.hertz.com

Index

See also Accommodations and Restaurant indexes, below.

Photo **Credits**